AFRICAN AMERICAN MOTHERS AND URBAN SCHOOLS

AFRICAN AMERICAN MOTHERS AND URBAN SCHOOLS

THE POWER OF PARTICIPATION

Wendy Glasgow Winters
HOWARD UNIVERSITY

LEXINGTON BOOKS
An Imprint of Macmillan, Inc.
NEW YORK

Maxwell Macmillan Canada
TORONTO

Maxwell Macmillan International
NEW YORK   OXFORD   SINGAPORE   SYDNEY

Library of Congress Cataloging-in-Publication Data

Winters, Wendy Glasgow.
  African American mothers and urban schools : the power of
participation / Wendy Glasgow Winters.
    p.   cm.
  Includes bibliographical references (p.   ).
  ISBN 0-669-28201-4
    1. Education—United States—Parent participation.   2. Afro
-American women—United States.   3. Education, Urban—United States
I. Title.
  LC225.3.W56   1993
  370.19′312′0973—dc20   93-11154
                                                              CIP

Lexington Books
An Imprint of Macmillan, Inc.
866 Third Avenue, New York, N.Y. 10022

Maxwell Macmillan Canada, Inc.
1200 Eglinton Avenue East
Suite 200
Don Mills, Ontario M3C 3N1

Macmillan, Inc. is part of the Maxwell Communication
Group of Companies.

Printed in the United States of America

printing number
1 2 3 4 5 6 7 8 9 10

To my mother, Gladys Russell, and the memory
of my late father, William Russell

Parents truly committed, by example, to education

Contents

Figures and Tables

Figures

Tables

Appendix Tables

Foreword

Wendy Winters has written a very important book. Most investigators have explored the benefits for students from parent participation in schools. Dr. Winters has explored the benefits for the parents themselves. The findings have implications far beyond the classroom and suggest ways that low income, often undereducated, and alienated people can gain the skills and confidence needed to participate in the economic and social mainstream of society.

I am not surprised by the findings, or the fact that Dr. Winters has written this book. I began my career in preventive psychiatry in 1968 in a school improvement program in New Haven, Connecticut, in which Dr. Winters served as the chief social worker. We both believed that adequate family functioning and good child rearing served to prepare students to succeed in school. This belief grew in large part from our own backgrounds.

We are both from working class African American families that were anchored in primary social networks of friend, kin, and supportive religious and social institutions. Despite limited education and denied opportunity when educated, our parents functioned well and enabled their children to get an education and enjoy professional careers. It is very likely that this background led to our first year program approach—a major effort to empower poorly functioning families.

During this time, Wendy spent a great deal of time outside of school working with five very needy families, with disappointing results. Issues of distrust and alienation from mainstream institutions and people could not be dealt with in the community. These poorly functioning families needed to interact with school people through normative, nonstigmatized activities. But there was no mutually respectful, helpful, and growth-producing way for the parents and school staff to interact. As a result of this experience, Dr. Winters concluded that we had to work with all parents in school, and that became her major focus in our second program year.

But it wasn't easy. Today it is widely accepted that parent participation in schools can be helpful to students. However in 1968 this was not the case. More than once we were told that parents didn't belong in schools. Some school people felt, "Parents should raise them and we will teach them." But as the parents got involved in supporting the social and academic program of the schools, the benefits to the staff, students, and eventually themselves became evident.

The governance and management structures and social climate that emerged in the schools permitted parents and staff to work together to plan and implement social and academic programs. They eventually developed a social program for a school year that included pot luck suppers, book fairs, spring flings, and a variety of activities that helped to create a good school climate. They also developed academic plans tailored to the needs of children in these schools. Attention was given to social as well as academic development, and parents were able to bring knowledge of their own children and the community to bear in a way that was helpful to school people. School people shared knowledge that was helpful to the parents.

In the beginning only the best functioning parents came forward. But as trust and mutual respect grew within the schools, the reputation of caring and concern grew beyond the schools. In what could be called a reversed domino effect, eventually even parents experiencing great difficulties began to turn to school social work and to other support and teaching staff for guidance and referrals. Parent turnout for the Christmas program went from 15 in the first year to 400 in the fourth, in a school with 350 students.

The collaborative effort provided the students with an environment of support for their overall development that eventually led to dramatically improved academic and social performance. The surprise effect was that, as the parents began to help their children, they began to help themselves. One day a long distance operator who was assisting me said that she had been a King School parent and that that experience had given her the confidence and skills needed to go out and take a job that previously she never would have thought herself capable of obtaining and holding. Other parents credited their school experiences for their improved functioning and employment. Some were inspired to go back and complete their own secondary education. Several went on to become professional people themselves.

The need to study what was going on with the parents was clear. Most adult education programs can reach only parents who are highly motivated and reasonably well-functioning in the first place. Our school program was motivating and providing skills to people who are often not served well in adult education efforts. But my first priority was to develop and disseminate our ideas and model of school improvement for students.

Over the years Wendy has continued to study and describe the parent participation aspect of schooling in a variety of ways. I am delighted that she has now looked at the benefit of parent participation for parents themselves. In elucidating the psychosocial dynamics involved, she has given practitioners a way to understand the benefits that will help them construct more effective school programs. In addition, this work should help policymakers facilitate parent participation. It will help us all understand how critical it is for everyone to have an opportunity to contribute in order to grow.

The value of Dr. Winters' work will increase as the findings are applied beyond the classroom and into housing projects, social organizations, and a variety of places where people—regardless of socioeconomic level, but particularly low income and often alienated—are trying to live and work together in complex systems. As Dr. Winters points out, participation is the essence of the democratic process. This book helps us understand how and why participation is important and beneficial, and how to facilitate it. Nothing could be more important.

James Comer

Preface

The release of this book parallels the critical attention being given to the public schools by our nation's leaders. The role of parents, especially the disadvantaged living in urban areas, continues to be scrutinized. This book explores parental participation in public schools as an opportunity for personal growth and empowerment and as a source of support for educational goals and needed resources.

Participation is viewed as an alternative to the alienation that so many less-favored individuals experience today. Personal stories and real school experiences of teachers, principals, parents, school social workers, school psychologists, guidance counselors, and children unfold in the context of informed social analysis. Qualitative and quantitative data give credence to the positive outcomes of parent-school collaboration. This book invites policymakers and school personnel to seek ways to engage parents.

In the first chapter, developmental, psychological, and sociological theories shed light on human potential and how this is related to participation, especially for African Americans. The meaning of competence for African Americans is explored in the context of a legacy of racism and second class citizenship.

The complexity and the promise of participation are considered in chapter 2. The participatory ethos as a common good in a democratic society is examined, as is direct participation in social institutions that influence our daily lives. Also reviewed are the impact of the language of parental involvement, the expectations of schools regarding the role of parents, and how the language and expectations have shifted in accordance with social change.

The relevance of the sociological construct of alienation and its dimensions (meaninglessness, normlessness, and powerlessness) for African Americans is discussed in chapter 3. The influence of sociocultural factors such as poverty, unemployment, drugs, violence, and racism is examined. A parent-school activity index was devised to explore the belief that a sense of alienation was reduced for mothers who actively participated in their children's school. The index was based on the pooled ratings of parent-school activities, by a principal, two teachers, two parents, a school-community aide, and a school social worker. The activities, issues, and process of devising the scale are presented in chapter 4.

Consistent with the spirit of the Baldwin-King School Program's commitment to engage parents in all facets of this special project, an evaluation of parents-as-consumers was undertaken, with parents as members of the research team. The issues raised are described in chapter 5, including the process of parent selection, training, and their contribution to developing and using the questionnaire.

In 1987, the study of participation and alienation was replicated. The outcome reveals interesting relationships between feelings of alienation and whether a mother's participation is high or low. Urban life and demographic variables play a significant role in the relationship between participation and alienation. Chapter 6 explores the influence of educational status and other demographic variables such as marital status and church attendance on the relationship between participation and a mother's sense of alienation.

Participation in the day-to-day life of the school provides opportunity for personal growth and empowerment. In chapter 7 the personal power that comes of participation is highlighted, noting the implications for regaining a community that will strengthen African American families and all of society.

Acknowledgments

This book about involvement and the promise and potential of people stems from a community of support, spanning more than two decades. Thank you to the many mothers who may recognize their stories although the names are disguised. I am grateful for the opportunity to have observed the growth of those of you who triumphed in your involvement.

Recognition is extended to the many classroom teachers who over the years continue to seek meaningful and creative ways to involve parents.

Dorothy Betty Gore, retired director of school social work services in the Milwaukee public schools, paved the way for the 1987 study, on which much of this book is based. Much cooperation and support was forthcoming from the superintendent and his office staff, the principals, teachers, and parents of the three schools implementing the pilot parent involvement project at that time. The input of three school social workers, Robert Kreuziger, Dorothy Parks, and David Weingrod was critical to the project.

I am grateful to my former colleague and collaborator Anthony Maluccio of the Boston College School of Social Work, who was instrumental in my focusing on competence and potential as the context in which to explore participation. An adept writer, Michael Winston's encouragement and confidence after reading an early draft of several chapters, provided essential motivation to pursue the project.

It has been my good fortune to have had administrators who supported and facilitated my work. In 1985 Jill Conway, then president of Smith College, provided me with a president's research award, that assisted with the Milwaukee study. In the 1970s, while at the Yale University Child Study Center, Albert Solnit, then director, mentored and encouraged my interest in and work with parents. My friendship with James Comer, director of the Baldwin-King School Program, now the School Development Program, spans more than two decades. His faith and dedication to parents and schools is reflected in his continued work. I cherish our continued association and his endorsement of my work. I cannot forget Joan Costello who suggested the parent-as-consumer evaluation and Carol Schraft, now a school principal, who assisted in the earlier study.

Completing this book, required the assistance of a number of people. A long time friend, Claire Gallant continues to influence the potential of parents although retired offered her good counsel and ideas. Another friend, Dolores Morris, one of six clinical administrators in the New York City Division of Special Education, commented on parts of the manuscript, exchanged ideas and offered references. I am particularly indebted to more recent friends and colleagues, Ann H. Brockenborough and Barry Rosenberg, who carefully read the entire manuscript and generously shared their knowledge.

James Rosenbaum of the Center for Urban Affairs and Policy Research at Northwestern University offered critical comments on part of the manuscript. My colleague at Howard University, Teresa Williams, was instrumental in suggesting and carrying out the statistical methodology and analysis used in the 1987 study. A patient teacher, I especially am grateful for the time she gave and her perseverance.

My associates in the Department of Sociology and Anthropology at Howard University who read and commented on parts of the manuscript were Florence Bonner, the chairwoman and Johnnie Daniel who encouraged making the book accessible to a wide audience. Thanks, also to Brunetta Wolfman, of George Washington University, who provided needed information.

I am grateful to Judy Williams, principal of the Shepherd School in Washington, D.C., who talked with me at length about her work with parents and who introduced me to Henrietta Ellis and Helease Hall, mothers who had worked with her in the early days of the Head Start program. Both are now employed in the District of Columbia public school system and were generous in giving their time to talk with me about their long careers in public education.

A special thanks for the research assistance provided by Krystal Knapp, Paula Snyder, Dora Stewart, Auria Styles, John Ukawuilulu, and Valencia Dillon.

Although the ideas and suggestions of many contributed to and are represented in this book, I take full responsibility for any errors.

I am blessed with my husband, Irving Winters, who encourages my accomplishments. Often, he would set aside his own demanding academic and research responsibilities to assist me. For a two year period, Irving was accepting of my virtual reclusiveness. Without his encouragement, nurturance, and belief in my ability, I could not have completed this book.

Lastly, I would like to thank Margaret Zusky for her faith in the project and Beverly Miller, whose copy editing taught me a great deal.

Introduction

P arents are the primary players in the daily drama of educating America's children. Yet in disadvantaged urban areas, they are generally unrecognized, unappreciated, often dismissed, and considered by the public school system as having little to offer. Within the parents of children attending public schools in the nation's inner cities rests untapped potential and resources. For schools that earnestly seek to realize their mission to educate America's poor inner-city children, the participation upon which this book is based becomes a viable option.

The African American mothers on whom this book focuses are poor. Many have had only limited education. A majority are single mothers receiving public assistance and raising their children in nonnurturing, threatening environments. By responding to opportunities programmed by schools committed to parent participation in day-to-day school life, these mothers are transformed and emerge with strengthened self-competence, new skills, and a determination to alter the direction of their lives. Some have gone on to further their own education. Others have become self-supporting through employment. Through sustaining and ongoing involvement in school and classroom life, these mothers become empowered advocates for their children's education. This growth carries over into other areas as they adopt wider societal goals. Still comparatively few in number, these women interact daily in inner-city schools across the country. Because a disproportionate number of African American males are caught in a spiral of drugs, violence, and incarceration, in the tradition of mothers in general, African American mothers are the principal participants in the education of their children.

Socioeconomic factors and traditional patterns of interaction frequently mitigate positive exchange between school personnel and their constituents in poor, urban communities. As a result, both, in defense, retreat. Parents avoid contact and are characterized as disinterested. Schools erect barriers that poor mothers perceive as insurmountable. Protected by the authority and power vested in their mission, schools operate routinely, while poor parents remain estranged.

An invitation to take part in a seemingly imposing institution sends a message of inclusivity through which much can be accomplished. Parent participation as conceived here refers to parents who become an integral part of their children's education. The presence of even a small, involved number of parents who assist teachers in the classroom or tutor children conveys a positive message to other parents that the school is accessible and to school personnel that parents are interested. An active parental presence affects the potential of participation in other significant ways. By example and by encouragement, parents who are involved stimulate increased attendance at school meetings and parent-teacher conferences, and they learn how to provide support at home that reinforces school expectations.

The mentoring and tutoring initiatives by professional and corporate groups that have surfaced in recent years are important contributions. African Americans and other empowered minorities and whites volunteer regularly in disadvantaged communities, making important connections with positive outcomes. This book, however, emphasizes the potential of engaging the disengaged by drawing upon and cultivating strength, building positive relationships, and developing determination as a result of experiencing responsibility for one's destiny. Participation has engendered a variety of results in the lives of these women. For many, the dysfunctional aspects of their lives are eradicated or at least mitigated, offering hope and a belief in the future.

A number of urban schools across the country have developed programs to facilitate parent involvement. The School Development Program spearheaded by Dr. James Comer is the arena in which the thesis of this book was developed. I served as chief social worker for the Baldwin-King School Program, forerunner of the School Development Program, at the Yale University Child Study Center from 1968 to 1975 with its emphasis on parent involvement. Earlier, from 1965 to 1968 as a school social worker in the Norwalk Public School System in Connecticut, I had participated in implementing the mandate to involve parents in Head Start.

Working with parents over the years in New Haven, I witnessed and shared the reality of their changed lives. Their struggles were real. Yet they were zealous in their commitment and remained determined to surmount seemingly impossible barriers. What became evident was their sense of ownership in educational issues. They did not shy away from problems but shared in their solution. As their hard-earned successes blossomed, their despair began to give way to deliberateness. Their overall demeanor was of reduced resignation. As the team undertook program evaluation, interest focused on exploring the essence of this change in the context of alienation. The sociological constructs of meaninglessness, normlessness, and powerlessness were used to evaluate quantitatively an individual's sense of alienation in terms of the effect of active participation in on-site school activities. Meaninglessness reflects a person's inability to understand what is going on in their world. The idea that it is acceptable to engage in socially disapproved behavior to realize one's goals is represented by normlessness. And powerlessness captures the defenselessness experienced when one has little or no control over his or her life chances. These three alienation constructs have been standardized on studies of African Americans (Bullough 1967; Middleton 1968; Willie 1968). Social scientists differ as to whether alienation is one-dimensional or patterned by discrete indicators, each in itself characterizing alienation, therefore, each construct was explored individually. The process of measuring participation is described at length in this book.

The Yale University Child Study Center and the New Haven Public School System joined in an initiative focusing on two elementary schools in predominately black neighborhoods. As we undertook evaluation of the Baldwin-King Program, we believed that parents as consumers of education, and program participants, should have an integral role in the evaluative process. At that time, in the early 1970s, any undertaking that was reminiscent of research or experimentation was suspect, and a potentially explosive tension existed between mainstream research universities in major cities and local minority communities. The idea to engage parents as informants and participants in the evaluation was consistent with the program's commitment to include parents.

The Baldwin-King School parent involvement program had been underway for more than six years when the initial evaluation study was undertaken. In order to explore differences in alienation and participation, parents in the Baldwin-King Schools and parents in a comparable elementary school that did not have a comprehensive school-wide parent involvement program were interviewed. U.S. census tract data verified the similarity of the schools in socioeconomic, e.g. income, and demographic characteristics, such as marital status and education (Winters 1975). In addition to the regular curriculum, there were other programmatic similarities among the schools since the control school had some federally funded programs that stipulated inclusion of parents. Given the small number of fathers in the sample, only responses from mothers were included in the study. In the 1975 study, mothers in the Baldwin-King School Program in comparison to control school mothers reject the statements reflecting meaninglessness and normlessness.

The ideas in this book are grounded in those early encounters and developed over the years of my consultation with school systems in New York, Louisiana, Massachusetts, North Carolina, Wisconsin and Washington, D.C. In 1985, I had the opportunity to work with Dorothy B. Gore, director of School Social Work Services, since retired from the Milwaukee Public Schools, who had obtained a small state grant to implement a pilot program focused on parent involvement in three elementary schools.

Compared to the 1975 study of the Baldwin-King Program with its broad base administrative, foundation, and university support the Milwaukee

Public Schools program between 1985 and 1987 was considered a modest endeavor. All three schools selected for the Milwaukee program were located in the inner city each with over 90 percent African American student populations. Over 80 percent of the students in one of the schools come from low-income families, and the student turnover rate at that approximates or exceeds 40 percent (*Milwaukee Journal* 1986). The other two schools have a similar profile.

In the years encompassing the pilot program the Milwaukee Public Schools had a number of educational initiatives focusing on improved educational performance. Each of the three schools was affiliated with one of these educational programs. One principal, a strong proponent of parent involvement in social and schoolwide activities prior to the pilot program, had instituted programs to generate parental support in improving attendance and focusing on homework. Yet after the pilot program had been underway for a year and a half, this principal reported that prior to the parent-school collaborative model, he had never had a core of regular parent volunteers such as the thirteen mothers who now consistently participated in on-going volunteer activities in the day-to-day life of the school (Annual Summary of Activities in Parent-School Collaboration Project 1986). The pilot program being carried out in the two other schools with state funding and central office endorsement, including the allocation of professional school social work staff to implement the initiative, strengthened this principal's long-time commitment and undertaking.

The 1987 study was based on the 1975 model. To explore the differences between alienation and participation, a total of 114 randomly selected mothers were interviewed in the spring of 1987 by a parent or a school social worker. Almost 80 percent were single heads of household. Of the remaining who were married, all of their spouses are employed, full or parttime. Of the less than 20 percent of the mothers who were employed, approximately half worked fulltime.

Statistical analysis of demographic variables and responses to the questionnaire revealed no significant differences between the three schools, and therefore they are treated here as a composite to compare high- and low-frequency participants. High-frequency participants are mothers who take part in on-site educational activities such as tutoring and assisting teachers in the classroom on a regular basis. Low-frequency participants attend school meetings and parent-teacher conferences or take part in other activities geared to the general school population and community at large. This book emphasizes participation in activities that directly influence the course of education. Both populations—high-frequency and low-frequency mothers—are located in the same school. The schools offer a number of more generalized social activities and information programs organized to attract a wide range of parents, thus tending to minimize the contrast between the two groups.

The schools examined in this research and others with similar objectives demonstrate that urban schools can successfully educate poor and minority children and benefit by engaging their parents in the process. These schools have implemented programs that eradicate the barriers between parents and schools.

For African Americans, education remains a powerful force in advancement and as a means of discarding the shackles of poverty and second-class status. Historically, blacks have viewed education as a major vehicle for improving the future of the race. In nineteenth-century America, black men were leaders of the movements promoting increased responsibilities and opportunities for males and females alike. Almost simultaneously, the voices of their female counterparts were added. Given that blacks have not had clear access to many mainstream societal goals, participation in the educational sector is one means of reducing the distance between a society and a primary sector of its constituents.

A growing body of scholarly research identifies the benefits of parent involvement for children and schools. Little has focused on the benefits for parents themselves. The basic premise of this book is that out of participation in school activities can come a sense of well-being, personal competence, and development with manifold benefits. The hope that so many continue to cherish is cultivated. Children, schools, and parents themselves emerge empowered.

1
Participation, Competence, and Interaction

In the ongoing national debate regarding educational outcomes, parent participation in schools occupies an interestingly nebulous position. The issue of the participation of parents surfaces even when it is not identified as central to the discourse. *A Nation at Risk* (1983), released a decade ago by the National Commission on Excellence in Education, acknowledges the primacy of parent participation in education, summoning parents to participate actively in the "work of the schools." But even as the clarion call issued in that document, participation remained formless. Implementation recommendations were specifically articulated for educational content, standards and expectations, basics, teaching, leadership, and fiscal support, while processes to implement parent participation remained unspecified.

The more recent executive initiative, *America 2000: An Education Strategy* (1991), misrepresents the intent of parent participation by defining it within the context of choice. Through the voucher system, the initiative equates parent participation with the purchasing of educational services, deemphasizing the expectation of participation in school activities.

Distinguishing Participation and Involvement

Often, *community control, decentralization, participation, parent involvement*, and *collaboration* are used interchangeably to refer to the interaction of parents and activist community members in school life. It is important to differentiate these terms conceptually.

In 1966, the ad hoc Parent Council in East Harlem, New York wanted more than involvement and participation in their children's schools. Their objective was a powerful role: control in the hiring and firing of teachers and administrators and control of the curriculum. Community control at the grass-roots level differs from decentralization, a bureaucratic strategy that delegates powers to an administrative structure closer to the local level.

1

Decentralization does not necessarily include the objective of engaging parents and community people in educational determinations (Ravitch 1974).

Participation, parent involvement, and *collaboration* connote a shared commitment. Power is omnipresent as an issue but remains more on the periphery of the sphere of interaction. School personnel maintain primary responsibility for carrying out school policy and processes and facilitating parent, community, and school collaboration. An articulation of goals and objectives includes clarifying boundaries. The intent and spirit conveyed by participation, involvement, and collaboration is that of mutuality. "Collaboration," in this context, "suggests that neither group can function effectively alone, that each group needs the cooperation of the other to carry out its mission. The sum of the collaboration is greater than the total of what each group could accomplish alone" (Winters and Easton 1983).

In the parlance of the school, participation generally encompasses a parent's assisting a child with homework, providing an atmosphere in which homework can be completed, and monitoring the completion of assignments. Suggestions from those in the educational sector to engage the child in conversation as to what took place in school that day is a form of participation that reinforces the school's goals and objectives and sends the message that school is endorsed in the home. Other aspects of participation include responding to school inquiries in a timely fashion, attending special school functions, and taking part in meetings with school personnel. Such expectations reflect a range of norms that pertain to all parents of school-aged children.

In the context of parent input in education, *participation* and *parent involvement* are used interchangeably. The two concepts share the expectation of an active parental role in the child's learning behaviors. However, in actuality they can connote different expectations and outcomes. Parent participation is but one aspect of parent involvement, which encompasses as well active participation in the day-to-day activities of the school. Moreover, each emphasizes distinct processes, evokes different expectations, and varies in accord with the needs of a particular school at a given time.

A number of elementary schools in the nation's inner cities have developed parent involvement programs to respond to the range of problems that they encounter. These initiatives include parents in their resolution and report positive outcomes (Comer 1980, 1986; Davies 1976). In Prince Georges County, Maryland, parents join the principal and teachers as members of the School Planning and Management Team (Mariott 1990). The Central Park East Elementary School in New York City links the principal, teachers, parents, and social workers to alleviate family problems that result in poor academic performance (Schorr 1989). At the Palmer School in Milwaukee, absenteeism was reduced when parent volunteers, guided by the school social worker, set up a telephone hot line and initiated and maintained contact with parents of children whose attendance was sporadic. But in spite of documented successful outcomes in terms of improved academic performance, mutually supportive interaction between parents and school personnel, and an increased sense of self among involved mothers, programs such as these remain few in number.

Involvement as used in this book refers to structural mechanisms put in place by the school that govern and orchestrate parent interaction in school organizations, processes, and activities. Through their participation, parents provide resources for the school and, in turn, learn new skills from the system. The direct service by parents affects the school in critical ways, positively influencing educational objectives and outcomes. Parents assist teachers in the classroom, tutor children, monitor playgrounds, hallways, or lunchrooms, and help out in the principal's office. They are included in managerial processes and in a number of additional ways.

Involvement connotes reciprocity between the individual and the social system of the school. *Reciprocal enculturation* refers to the process whereby new cultural patterns are acquired by both systems, family and school, as they develop and mature, and each can be endowed with new energy that changes its configuration. Involvement captures for disadvantaged parents the ethos embodying the volunteerism that for decades has brought countless numbers of citizens to work in schools and hospitals (Alden 1979). Time, commitment, and personal responsibility in day-to-day activities are key dimensions. Greenberg's (1975) conceptualization of participation as an intense experience in terms of time, commitment, and energy occurring within a narrowly specified latitude of decisions complements participation and involvement as carried out in this study.

Differences in parent-school interaction has to do with where families live, cultural and income differences, and children's age and educational level. At a parent-teacher cooperative school in Salt Lake City that has endured for over a decade, public school personnel continue to move beyond customary bureaucratic boundaries in their interaction with parents. Parents have a definitive voice in the hiring of teachers and share with school personnel discretionary responsibility in selecting textbooks (Johnston and Slotnik 1985). This example of interaction represents one variety of innovative alliances between schools and families.

Parent involvement is especially important in schools in which parents, for a myriad of social, economic, and psychological reasons, are less motivated and empowered to involve themselves in their children's education. Moreover, in more affluent suburban schools, there is a better fit between the values and expectations of school personnel and the families they serve. Schools where increasing numbers of children whose families' incomes fall below the poverty line have inadequate resources. Given poor academic performance and marginal literacy, inner-city students continue to lag far behind students living in middle- and upper-class suburbs. In this climate of failure, engaging and reaching out to parents proves difficult. Yet both outreach and sustaining meaningful contact are critical in view of the enormity of the problems urban schools face and the urgent need to engage parents in efforts to educate their children in adverse circumstances.

A few inner-city schools have experienced success in involving parents, but others have given up, their efforts rebuked, politicized, or sabotaged. Schools that fail to involve parents are in the majority and maintain that their inability to engage poor urban parents is due to the parents' disinterest and lack of commitment. These parents remain alienated and see no opportunity for their inclusion. They feel they lack the knowledge and ability that would equip them to deal effectively with schools, which they experience as unapproachable bureaucracies (Heid and Harris 1989). In retreat, their defiance is reinforced.

Unless parent involvement is sanctioned and institutionalized at the administrative level and schools are provided with the requisite support, a program's continuation is in jeopardy. This is not to suggest that state or federal directives mandate participation but rather they provide guidelines and incentives designed to encourage localities to develop programs that fit local needs and populations. The Comer School Development Program received early supplemental funding from Yale University and the Ford Foundation and continues to have ongoing financial backing from the Rockefeller Foundation to ensure a partnership with local school systems. The Schools Reaching Out project sponsored by the Institute for Responsive Education focuses on neighborhood school programs emphasizing participation of principals, teachers, and parents to promote ownership and by so doing support their endurance (Davies 1990). Ultimately institutionalization, whereby the locality assumes responsibility for community- and parent-based programs, is anticipated.

A National Incentive

No single or simple measure will resolve the issues plaguing public schools in poor urban communities. The national government has a responsibility to lead the way for more equitable distribution of resources. Resolutions must be comprehensive, drawing on national, local, and individual potential and resources. A national strategy that focuses on compiling and analyzing processes and data regarding public school programs that have proved successful in inner cities throughout the nation is needed.

Lessons learned from locally implemented models are applicable throughout the nation. Following decades of a research and design intervention approach, these programs demonstrate that urban school systems cannot undertake substantive enduring programs of parent involvement without outside support. Parent involvement is a complex and complicated process that evolves over time, becoming a key element of other processes in the school, before leading to long-term institutionalized commitment. Implementation cannot be left to nonprofessionals. Sustained leadership, fiscal support, on-going training, and redevelopment are key factors.

Leadership is needed on the federal level to develop policies, implement procedures, and evaluate outcomes. A nationally endorsed incentive, with requisite resources, could operate from centers in state and local municipalities to develop existing resources. An initial and primary function would be to gather, assess, and disseminate information regarding prevailing programs. This is not to suggest that fixed models would be transferable to urban schools. Rather local and regional satellite centers, acting as a repository, able to identify expertise and resources, would function to motivate and assist inner-city schools to develop and implement parent involvement programs in keeping with their own needs. Such an initiative would encourage state and local municipalities to engage local diverse community representation in concert with professionals in articulating problems and planning strategies. Parent involvement would be a critical element.

In this approach, information and support must be readily available to local school systems. New parent involvement programs can use existing ones as guides and thus avoid the "reinvent-the-wheel" mentality that is a costly by-product of the cherished self-determination and individualism ideal.

The lack of involvement of urban city parents in their children's schools is just one of the many problems urban schools face and is often overshadowed by more highly visible problems. Certainly parent involvement is not a solution to all of the problems of urban schools—poor academic performance, absenteeism, homeless families, inadequate supplies, deteriorating buildings, staff reductions, low teacher morale, and violence—but it can reduce the debilitating aspects of a number of problems.

One of the less visible outcomes of parent involvement are the intrinsic benefits that can accrue for parents themselves. The focus in this book is on that potential in the context of pursuing the scope of parent participation and parent involvement.

The Promise of Participation

Parent involvement in education, first mandated federally in Head Start programs in the mid-1960s, has taken on a number of configurations that are different from policies and practices in earlier times, when the parents' role was confined to conferences with teachers, attending school performances or social functions, and participating in fund-raising activities. Today, parent involvement spans a range of school-based functions and activities, including participation on advisory or governing boards and serving as teacher assistants, playground or lunchroom attendants, and classroom monitors.

The structure and forms participation takes and the analysis of educational costs and benefits dominate the parent involvement discourse. There is documentation of improvement in academic performance as a by-product of parent involvement (Henderson 1987) but little empirical research that focuses on the benefits of participation for parents themselves and how their participation benefits schools and ultimately advances societal goals.

For parents, the participatory process offers opportunity for personal and psychological development. In one study, Parker, Piotrkowski, and Peay (1987) noted that mothers who participated in Head Start–sponsored educational activities demonstrated an increased sense of personal well-being. Active parental participation in the educational sector can reduce alienation and generate competence through the development of individual capabilities that foster fulfillment of personal and societal goals. This prospect offers an opportunity to engage urban African American, poor, and/or minority parents whose day-to-day functioning is external to or on the periphery of meaningful interaction with mainstream society.

For the school, interaction with parents extends the school's capacity to understand and appreciate the values and culture of the families and to meet the educational needs of children they serve more effectively. Parents, having been acknowledged and perhaps even appreciated, will be more likely to support the educational program and further their children's performance. Professional school personnel develop new skills as they learn to negotiate in different ways and are challenged to utilize and nurture resources they never before considered. James Comer's work in New Haven, Connecticut, Prince Georges County, Maryland, and in another one hundred schools across the nation is testimony to the positive outcomes of parent involvement for schools and teachers. Schools affiliated with the Schools Reaching Out project report advancement in parent-school interaction.

Parent involvement in programming for the developmentally, emotionally, and socially disabled is mandated, but the mandate does not extend to the general educational program. And even in special education, school systems continue to struggle with implementing parent involvement.

In the early nineteenth century, it was generally accepted that parents endorsed school values and expectations that reflected wider societal imperatives. During that time, the socialization function of the school and family were closely aligned. Following World War II, with the large-scale migration to cities and shifts in population, the configuration of the school population changed, with increasing numbers of children attending schools located in urban areas. School personnel, teachers, and other middle-class socioeconomic groups moved to the suburbs. Migration in and out of the urban areas shifted the population attending urban public schools. Changes in industry and light manufacturing affected the economic well-being of the cities. By the 1960s, the country responded with antipoverty programs and initiatives directed to the educational sector. Under the aegis of Head Start, an early education intervention program, parent involvement was a requirement for schools in rural areas, small towns, and cities with disadvantaged minority and low socioeconomic status populations.

Urban Realities

Evidence of the deterioration in the infrastructure of urban centers abounds. Thousands of children of homeless families attend school sporadically or not at all. If attending, they are unable to bond successfully with teachers and bear the burden of negative social and educational outcomes. Inner-city life is characterized by the insidious prevalence of drugs with the concomitant violence, an increasing drop-out rate, functional illiteracy, poor academic performance, parental apathy, and a mounting number of teenage parents. How can such environments engender strength or lead to growth?

Many African American families and children who live under such seemingly unbearable conditions can and do survive and lead productive lives. However, a disproportionate number fall victim to the squalor and its erosive effects. Parents in this social system range from those unable to provide adequate shelter, food, and clothing for their offspring to the working poor, who hold two to three jobs and still are unable to make ends meet. The reality of high unemployment in urban areas and the unequitable number of unemployed ethnic minorities is well documented. Single-parent families have become the norm, and teenage mothers are rapidly on the rise (Edelman 1988; Schorr 1989; Wilson 1987).

In a majority of inner-city schools, each day teachers enter dilapidated and substandard buildings, go to overcrowded classrooms, distribute defaced or outdated textbooks, face hungry and undernourished children, and are expected to carry out a centrally mandated, often irrelevant, curriculum. Even in schools with adequate facilities, supplies, and resources, chronic absenteeism, poor academic performance, severe behavioral problems, disillusioned teachers, and discouraged parents are common.

Middle-class African Americans have joined the exodus of the white middle class from the nation's central cities. Working-class families are part of this exodus, leaving inner-city communities bereft of families who demonstrate self-sufficiency, direction, and purpose in their daily lives by going to work, reflecting pride by maintaining their homes, and participating in church or community activities. The fastest-growing populations in an increasing number of cities are poor African Americans and ethnic minorities. Given patterns of historical racism and structural economic conditions that limit opportunity and access, African Americans, while only 12 percent of the nation's population, account for almost one-third of the nation's poor. Although token gains have been made in the work force, with African Americans occupying such positions as vice presidents in Fortune 500 companies and in being represented in professional, technical, and entrepreneurial circles, the median wage for black Americans remains 43 percent lower than that of white Americans. African American male unemployment at 15 percent is twice that of white males, and 42 percent of black males between the ages of sixteen and nineteen do not have jobs (Bureau of Labor Statistics 1992). The criminal justice system lays claim to an astonishingly disproportionate number of black males between the ages of eighteen and twenty-four: 25 percent. Never-married black females head families in which approximately 44 percent of African American children under the age of eighteen live (U.S. Bureau of the Census 1990). Children within these environments make up a disproportionate percentage of the population of inner-city schools. As products of these realities, many are burdened with deficits from birth.

Women as Primary Participants

Traditionally in America, it is women who have maintained primary contact with schools. For decades, Parent Teachers Associations (PTA) across the country have been headed by mothers. This interaction with schools differs from the model of collaboration on which this book is based.

The role of women in or in behalf of schools is a long-standing and sanctioned convention (Lightfoot 1978), but for single mothers in the inner city, with a legacy of welfare dependency, powerlessness, and accompanying despair, this expectation can be but one more burden. Yet even in the most stressful environments, people can have positive experiences that produce strengths. In spite of the desolate neighborhoods, deteriorating schools, disillusioned teachers, desperate parents, and educationally abandoned children, resources exist within the environment and, particularly, within the parents themselves and can be drawn upon to alter prevalent conditions significantly. The rapidly changing contours and context of America's cities and neighborhoods are readily reflected in the problems schools face. Educational responses must change. A major thesis of this book emphasizes the role and use of environmental resources and the inherent strength in people in the pursuit of personal growth and societal goals. The positive outcomes for mothers who sustained participation in Head Start activities for a year, is living evidence of this promise (Parker et al. 1987).

"Taking Part," Adaptation, and Competence

Participation in schools evolves as a conduit for developing personal competence. The act of taking part in school activities can generate positive attitudes and competent behaviors. Adaptation, competence, and mastery of the social environment are primary themes underlying this book. Adaptation and the development of competence occur in the context of interaction with the environment. Viewed from an ecological perspective, human beings as living systems are propelled toward growth, development, and self-determination and are inclined to seek increased autonomy. White (1974) posits adaptation as a dynamic process in which people continuously reach for an acceptable compromise with external forces. In the process of adaptation, they assimilate new experiences and skills, fostering psychological growth and development.

In formulating his theory of competitive motivation, White (1959, 1963) departs from psychological and psychoanalytic theories that connect motivation to instinctual drives and the reduction of tension. Rather, he defines competence in the context of biological and psychological functioning representing the person's capacity to negotiate the environment, both physical and social, effectively (Maluccio 1981). In the sphere of human interaction, at least two individuals become engaged in negotiation. When school personnel are culturally competent—i.e., aware of, and appreciate contributions of those who are different, and able to take appropriate action—they are more likely to invite parents to negotiate. When parents are competent, they may even initiate the process of negotiation.

Given the restricted and barren environments of America's inner cities, often there appears little to entice or challenge individuals who can barely eke out an existence. Yet each day these citizens use their repertoire of available skills in their quest to satisfy the needs of their families. Among this group of families is a range of skills and potential for development. Some people require only minimal stimuli to be propelled on a growth-producing path. Such is the case of seven-year-old Robby's mother who, after getting him and his three younger siblings ready for school, assists a fifth-grade teacher daily with a class of thirty-five students, ranging in ages ten to thirteen, a majority of them frustrated by their own academic problems.

Other mothers are stymied by the inertia that accompanies powerlessness and can barely provide for the day-to-day needs of their families. Yet they too have skills available for development. Withdrawn, despondent, and overwhelmed Lowanda Henderson, a twenty-year-old single mother of a six and a seven year old, started her involvement in her children's school by folding notices and distributing mail as an assistant in the school's main office. Each year she took on new tasks as she accumulated new skills and took advantage of training opportunities. Two years later, she qualified for the salaried position of school clerk.

Often the essence for potential growth is overshadowed by the drabness and alienation tightly woven in the fabric of a meager, seemingly hopeless existence. However, individual advancement such as Ms. Henderson's is replicated time and again across the country (Marriott 1990; Pennekamp and Freeman 1988; Schorr 1989; Winters and Maluccio 1988). Competence that comes about from repeated experiences of effectiveness unfolds as a promising concept in exploring participatory outcomes in public schools.

Competence and African Americans

Social and behavioral scientists across disciplines in sociology, anthropology, social work, and psychology identify competence as a basic factor in self-realization and of primacy in personal development. Perusal of the scholarly literature illustrates much variation on the competence theme. In this book, the concept of competence provides the context for analyzing the reciprocal interactions that occur between parents and the school. From an ecological systems perspective, the school is one of numerous social systems (family, neighborhood, workplace, and health clinics, among others) that operate simultaneously within the social sphere. In each sphere, an individual assumes a number of roles, each bearing a particular status within the hierarchy. Human resiliency enables individuals to negotiate a myriad of, and sometimes conflicting, statuses and roles.

Inkeles (1966) defines competence as an individual's ability "to attain and perform in three {distinct} statuses." First, individuals function in the status normally assigned by society. *Assigned status* refers to the position to which an individual enters by virtue of circumstance of birth, such as minority status based on skin color. The second dimension refers to the repertoire of statuses or positions available in a person's social system to which one may reasonably aspire. For example, African Americans and other minorities who are born restricted to the limitations that accompany darker or different skin color can have aspirations that exceed their assigned status. Third are those statuses that come about as individuals realize dreams and assume new roles. The critical aspect of Inkeles' formulations is the suggestion and recognition that new roles are realistic and attainable. Opportunity and access are vital to this conceptualization. Significant numbers of African Americans have risen and achieved all three hierarchically ordered statuses, in the process shedding the legacy of poverty and its accompanying roles defined by powerlessness and despair. Nevertheless, the legacy of poverty and hopelessness remains a reality to disproportionate numbers of African Americans (Blackwell 1985; Edelman 1988; Wilson 1987).

Through anthropological lens, Gladwin (1967) views social competence as emerging from an individual's ability to fulfill societal requirements and achieve personal goals. Interaction in the social system provides the individual with feedback and reinforcement, an essential motivating force. In the social system of the school, parents receive formal feedback regarding their children's academic performance in the form of report cards and verbal praise or reprimands. Informal feedback includes comments about clothing, personal, or family attributes. Feedback from school personnel can be a demoralizing rather than motivating force, frequently the case involving disadvantaged inner-city families. The self-fulfilling prophecy discourse by Rist (1970) substantiates the devastating outcome of negative reinforcement. Comer (1980, 1988) comments on how teachers and school personnel in their own frustration continue inadvertently to discourage or send messages to children and their parents that serve to minimize performance and potential. When a teacher rather innocently asks a child why his or her parents did not attend back-to-school night, the child absorbs the blame and believes something is wrong with his or her parents and self. Adding her voice to this theme, Lightfoot (1978) notes how teachers frequently view black parents through distorted lens; they misconstrue their behavior, consequently labeling them as neglectful and ignorant and, as such, devaluing of education.

Although traditionally teachers hold statuses of higher rank and thus positions of power, feedback is not unidimensional. Students and parents utilize an informal system in evaluating school personnel. Although this evaluation is not readily available and officially solicited, it can serve as useful feedback. In the spirit of accountability, consumers of public education should have a forum for providing feedback. Public schools in America continue to struggle with how to make this concept work in a manner acceptable to both school personnel and parents. Parent involvement, not unrelated to the issue of accountability, utilizes an approach that seeks to become more aligned with and central to the educational process itself. Opportunities for mutual feedback are a natural outcome of a participatory environment.

Social competence merges into three distinct but interacting components, notes Gladwin (1967): (1) the capacity to learn or to use different behaviors to realize goals, (2) the ability to negotiate and utilize resources available within a social system, and (3) the use of knowledge or skill to assess accurately the social reality. Hence, competence is generated and revitalized by personal activity, which can produce favorable or unfavorable outcomes. These propositions suggest that the resources, supports, and opportunities for goal attainment that excite and keep alive a sense of hope must be available in the social environment. In each of these theoretical formulations, the environment looms paramount.

In articulating developmental tasks in the process of assimilation of immigrants, Dahl (1961) isolates the emergence of self-confidence as a powerful social characteristic that is an outcome of participation in the social environment. Originators of Head Start saw and emphasized the importance of environment by focusing on environmental enrichment for the whole child, encompassing health, nutritional, cognitive, social, and emotional needs within the context of strong family involvement (Zigler and Valentine 1979). Yet even now, over twenty years later, resources, access, and supports available in the social environment remain unattainable for the majority of African Americans. Accompanying the motivation to fulfill basic physiological requirements of food, shelter, and clothing, human beings strive for security, love, belonging, and self-esteem. Self-esteem refers to the intrinsic value or worth an individual attaches to himself or herself as a person, experiencing feelings of self-confidence and self-approval, in contrast to feelings of self-rejection or self-dissatisfaction. Self-esteem emanates from and is manifested in achievement, adequacy, mastery, competence, independence, confidence, and self-actualization and is in part dependent on the role models whom individuals internalize, usually parents and significant others.

Emphasizing the interrelatedness of the social environment and personal development, White (1974) concurs that competence, an aspect of a strengthened ego, is the product of an accumulation of a person's effective interactions with the environment. As an ongoing developmental task throughout the life cycle, achieving competence is a requisite for self-esteem (Erikson 1968; Gilligan 1982). The self-competent person emerges as possessing self-confidence in his or her ability to make decisions and trust his or her own judgment. Participation in school activities provides a forum for decision making and the testing out and refinement of one's judgment that cultivates social competence. For example, in a number of special education programs, previously uninvolved parents have emerged empowered as advocates, volunteers, or peer counselors (Pennekamp and Freeman 1988). Not only does their participation in the process of stock taking and strategic planning contribute to personal development; it is also beneficial for the school in that the participants as consumers join with the school in the quest for mutually determined goals.

Competence also is represented as an integrative concept involving both intrinsic and extrinsic motivation (Smith 1968). From the holistic perspective of social psychology, social roles, social skills, and personal abilities combine as an individual seeks goals beneficial for self and society. A number of factors in both the social world and the individual's personal life influence competent human functioning. For example, with children this involves motivating and mentoring in behalf of self-empowerment. For adults, ongoing growth-producing and challenging experiences can foster self-actualization. In emphasizing the organism-person, Smith includes a person's sense of efficacy in controlling his or her destiny, a belief in hope, and respect for an acceptance of self. This conceptualization embodies the American value of individualism, extending to the basic level of family functioning and concern with the welfare and educational survival of one's offspring.

Although one-third of the nation's African Americans live in poverty (U.S. Census 1991), are effectively denied access to opportunities, and are vulnerable to the disillusionment and despair that accompany a substandard existence, Blackwell's (1985) research leads him to conclude, "To be black means for many an uncontestable commitment to free enterprise and the Protestant work ethic not undistinguishable from those who share such beliefs among the white ruling class" (p. 3). It is not surprising that African Americans embrace these values. Even among the poorest, most destitute families, there are parents who get their children to school and respond to the school's efforts to engage them. Although the input of these parents may be marginal, their inclination to embrace the school and its goals is present. The importance of this must not be minimized in the wake of the pervasive apathy, uniformed defensiveness, and alienation that engulf this population. Historically, one of the main functions of public education in America has been socialization of heterogeneous ethnic and religious groups (Mennerick and Najafizadeh 1987). In the context of social policy analysis, the intent of school desegregation legislation was to incorporate black Americans into mainstream society (Braddock 1985). Yet this is still not a reality for African Americans who remain socially dislocated and outside the boundaries of sanctioned participation in American society.

Through day-to-day experiences, people can become prepared for participation in the wider social system. A belief in human beings as productive, contributing participants is at the core of this expectation. With its emphasis on task achievement and acquisition of motor skills, developmental theory provides another lens of the essence of ego mastery, and it too resonates with the participatory ethos. An individual's ability to gain control of his or her environment is a significant indicator of ego mastery and competence. People gain ego mastery by accumulating a fair share of successful experiences, becoming motivated toward increased maturity. Within this dynamic process, the ego becomes stronger through the expansion of, reliance on, and approval of self (Wasserman 1979).

Socialization, in the context of parent involvement in schools, enables parent participants to give fuller exposure to their abilities and capabilities. African American mothers with minimal education and skills who initially present as withdrawn, depressed, and with low self-esteem often are perceived as lacking motivation. However following substantial participation in school activities, the potential for motivation that has been lying dormant is stimulated, and these women's lives and outlook are radically altered as they develop competencies and skills (Parker, Piotrkowski, and Peay 1987). The mothers acquire mature and adult characteristics as they become more active, independent, self-directed, and able to undertake multiple tasks and adopt long-term goals. They emerge empowered and able to interact with school personnel from a more equal position rather than one that is subordinate (Greenberg 1975). Instead of being patronized, they are consulted. Instead of being left out, they are included.

So often alienated and rendered powerless, African Americans, the poor, and those with limited access have little opportunity to experience control of their destiny and their potential. Rather, they are beholden to the landlord and the welfare and health care bureaucracies, which are vital to their daily existence. Socialized and silenced to reticence and often embarrassment, these parents, taking their cues from society, blame themselves for their children's inadequacies and failures. A cloak of reticence and blame shields them from learning the primary causes and implication of school failure, and thus their powerlessness is perpetuated (Fruchter 1984). Traditional patterns of participation for this population will not suffice. The variations among black families and their subcultures are challenging schools to alter the patterns of interaction. Teachers are being confronted to examine the ways in which they respond and relate to children who deviate from the mainstream. As schools redefine and recast their goals and missions, the values, attitudes, and behavior representative of their constituents must be acknowledged and included in the undertaking. Through participation, the capacity of African Americans and other less favored minorities to make worthwhile contributions to society can be expanded as they are enriched and revitalized by the society that was intended to serve them (Winters and Easton 1983).

When a belief prevails that the adaptive fit between people and their environments can be modified, the focus is on the reciprocal process, with the goal being to improve the human condition and simultaneously maximize human potential and improve environments (Germain and Gitterman 1980). Reciprocal enculturation infuses all components of the social system (family, schools, community, nation) with energy and new resources and brings about new attitudinal and behavioral patterns and unanticipated outcomes. Benefits for society are innumerable. This conceptualization is essential to the positive participatory outcomes in reciprocal parent-school collaboration. Such interaction is reported to have a favorable effect on school climate, teacher morale, parent cooperation, student behavior, and academic performance (Comer 1988; 1986; Marcus 1984; Narvaez 1984; Rosenberg 1984).

Personal self-confidence, defined as effective interaction with the environment, is fundamental to continuous development in adults. White's (1959) early formulation and Maluccio's (1981) more recent work informs the belief that experiences borne of participation can unearth individual potential. Ecological competence as played out in day-to-day existence considers the whole person—his or her skills, individual qualities, and expectations—in interaction with the environment.

Parent involvement in schools can perpetuate self-competence and help prepare individuals for participation in mainstream society with a reasonable opportunity for success. Through participation in activities and specialized functioning within organizations and by cooperating, pooling resources, sharing information, and engaging in mutual helping relationships, individuals grow and develop mastery (Mechanic 1974).

A mother who walked her children to school each morning was disturbed by the aggressive and potentially dangerous behavior that occurred on the school grounds before the school doors were opened. Children would push one another and fights would break out. After attending a number of school meetings, in which she learned that other mothers were assisting teachers in school and taking on a range of responsibilities, she quietly suggested that the school might set up a monitoring system. With some hesitation, she agreed to work with several other mothers in thinking through a plan. Together they solicited volunteers and set up an ongoing operation, with great success.

Parents have been successful in reaching out and engaging other parents when the efforts of school professionals have been ineffectual. Repeatedly,

Melba Morgan did not keep several appointments with the principal regarding her son's disruptive behavior. After two mothers from the school visited and talked with her a number of times, she agreed to accompany them to school and with their support met with the principal.

By being involved in educational activities at schools, parents become motivated, seek to maximize their strengths, and discover and use their potential. Participation can advance the discovery of individual competence and promote collective ego mastery among a group. I am not suggesting that participation in schools will cure all the ills besetting poor, apathetic, and powerless African Americans, but it is one way to bring alienated minorities in harmony with the values, opportunities, and norms associated with American life. If environments are to be supportive, it must be conveyed to participants that they are valued and esteemed members of a reciprocal system that provides emotional and concrete support (Germain 1988). In nurturing environments in which participants can learn new skills, acquire knowledge and information, and try on new roles, human potential can be advanced.

Cultural Conditioning: African Americans and Schools

Members of subcultures straddle two and sometimes multiple worlds. Included in this configuration are the individual's culture of reference, a subculture; the dominant or mainstream culture; and other subcultural entities that can emerge when different cultural groups interact. In a climate of pluralism, a range of cultural patterns, values, and perceptions is considered valid, although they may vary with those of the majority culture. Minority group members in America are socialized within a distinct subcultural context and at the same time are exposed to and socialized in the context of the dominant society. Ideally, the uniqueness of each subculture is recognized in the socialization process, yet it is expected that subcultural groups will function within the boundaries of the mainstream society, follow its conventions, and adopt its normative patterns and values. Cultural consistency in America connotes sharing a common language, similar behavior patterns, and a set of core values grounded in democracy and capitalism (Braddock 1985). The public school, as an agent of socialization, joins the family and religious groups in carrying out this function. Didactic instruction and patterning of behavior in schools serve the socialization process, which ideally respects the integrity of the values of the subcultural minorities.

Given historical racism and socioeconomic differences, a majority of educational leaders and public school personnel share neither the culture nor the values of the population they serve. In discussing root causes of school failure, Fruchter (1984) identifies cultural distance and dissonance as a critical factor. The argument is not that schools with large minority populations should be managed by minorities but that minority representation in leadership and teaching roles is essential in the educational and socialization process. Children and their families must see and work with individuals from their own cultural or ethnic group in positions of responsibility and power, carrying out critical and valued societal roles. Understanding, perspective, and presence can be brought to the educational process by school personnel who share the cultural background of the student population and value that background as useful and valid (Comer 1985, 1989; Ogbu 1988; Slaughter 1988). Certainly even within racial and ethnic groups, class or socioeconomic differences can be divisive.

The emphasis in this book is not solely on the enculturation that occurs involving disparate cultural groups but on the reciprocity occurring between two systems in transaction—the environment, with inherent physical and social properties, and human interactions (Germain 1988). Enculturation is different from socialization; it connotes the acquisition of new cultural patterns by systems that have reached apparent maturity (Theodorson and Theodorson 1969). In this book, the distinction is important because emphasis is on how participation influences positive changes and fosters growth and development in both human and environmental systems even when they have endured decades of inequities and appear fully developed. Schools, administrators, teachers, professional and support staff, students, and parents, as members of unique social systems, are all subject to change and development. As distinctive social environments, each school, with its own physical environment, specified goals, and variations in role groups, is made up of a number of systems in interaction with one another while interacting simultaneously with wider social, political, and economic forces. Each school has its own character, rhythm of interaction, expectations, values, and code of behavior—indeed, as Sarason (1982) posits, a culture of its own.

Contrasting Examples

On a walk through the Evans Elementary School in a northeastern inner city, one notes pictures of African American scientists, teachers, doctors, and engineers gracing the walls of the corridors. Hallways are free of litter. Children walk through the halls with a sense of purpose, direction, and mutual respect. A look through a classroom door will reveal small groups of children clustered around a science project, while others concentrate on a reading lesson with the teacher. A little farther down the corridor, a distraught fifth-grade boy defiantly avoids the gaze of the principal as he is being chastised. One is moved by the patience and gentle manner the principal displays in handling this youngster. His words are stern but send a clear message of belief in the boy's potential to exercise self-control and to assume responsibility for more acceptable behavior.

Five miles away in the same inner city, bedlam reigns at Locust Avenue

Elementary School. Children on their way to the auditorium push and shove one another, and a fistfight breaks out. Corridors are strewn with discarded papers, candy wrappers, and other refuse. New graffiti appears on a wall still bearing faint traces of graffiti previously washed away. In a classroom obviously disrupted by the din in the hallway, an overwhelmed teacher continuously yells, "Take and stay in your seats," while being ignored by most of the class.

The student population in both schools is majority African American and Hispanic. Such extremes exist in all inner cities. Although the two schools described here obviously differ from one another, the contrast is even greater when comparisons are made with schools located in suburban areas. American blacks, on the average, still receive poorer-quality education from the nation's school system than do whites (Kozol 1991; Murphy 1990). The nonwhite population in America, a substantial and continually expanding proportion of the populace, remains differentiated from the mainstream in critical ways.

The character and culture of public schools reflect ever-changing social and economic conditions:

- With the advent of serial and step families, parent-teacher conferences and back-to-school nights have taken on different configurations.

- Two career families and single-parent households have increased demands on school systems to provide day care through extended elementary school day and year programs and to provide tutoring and enrichment activities.

- A school in the Midwest established a school-based telephone network operated by parent volunteers to monitor latchkey children until their parents arrived home. Because of this service, the school building now remains open until six o'clock.

- In a departure from customary practice, parents of children in neighborhood schools in Washington, D.C., New Haven, Connecticut, and New York City voted that children be required to wear school uniforms. Their goal was to offset the unwholesome competitiveness and emphasis on trendy clothing that preoccupies so many young people.

- With the growing number of teenage parents, especially single mothers, schools are faced with adolescent parents who have unmet educational and social needs as well as a lack of parenting skills. In response, schools offer parenting workshops during the school day. Space and supervision for younger siblings is often required while mothers participate in school-sponsored programs.

The constancy of student turnover in schools located in urban areas affects other children in the classroom, as it does teachers' planning, time, and patience. Chronic absenteeism and tardiness have resulted in some schools altering the pattern of the school day. The increasing number of children of homeless families are leaving administrators and teachers frustrated in their efforts to respond to these very needy children, whose adjustment and ability to develop educationally are seriously affected by their tragic existence. Their classmates, whose own lives are often marginal, are not left unaffected by the grim reality of the lives of their homeless peers. The extent to which the many variables and potential obstacles are identified and challenged will determine the school's ability to meet the educational needs of students and the wider participatory needs of the community.

Schools and Social Change

Schools are at the center of the political and passionate debate regarding AIDS and in order to be in compliance with legal mandates seek ways to accommodate school-age children afflicted with the disease. School-based health clinics are being reorganized to respond to the drug and alcohol epidemic and to the increased level of sexual activity among teenagers. The availability of information concerning maternity alternatives and the distribution of condoms in elementary as well as in junior and senior high schools generate heated debate among school personnel, students, families, politicians, and the clergy.

Public schools in inner cities are besieged by the violence that is over taking the city streets. Gang violence is played out on school property and even in classrooms. Youngsters walking to and from school are vulnerable to drug-related violence. The profit-making sector has targeted bulletproof clothing for children as a viable market. A number of urban school districts are instituting sophisticated security measures and holding workshops to train school personnel to respond to the threat of violence.

As increasing minority populations from Third World countries settle in cities, public schools are challenged to respond to populations with different cultures, languages, values, and norms. Socioeconomic and political forces impinge on families and children, affecting them and the transaction with public schools. As parties to these transactions, schools are affected by the interaction and become altered in the process.

Ordinarily when we think of public schools as institutions with socialization goals and objectives to foster growth and development, children, not parents, come to mind. With increasing numbers of teenage parents, high dropout rates among urban youth, adult illiteracy, and persistent alienation, producing good citizens who are equipped with the appropriate values, perceptions, and normative behavior to make a positive contribution to society must remain a central function of public schools. Schools cannot accomplish this goal without the meaningful input and ongoing cooperation of families. Parents have a primary and vital role in the socialization of their children. Yet the complexities of modern society have complicated this process for many parents, especially those who suffer disadvantage and live in abject circumstances. Public schools must find ways to collaborate with parents and draw them into the educational process.

Public opinion polls reveal that increasing numbers of Americans believe that the public educational system is failing its students and thus its families. Such beliefs are substantiated by reports from the corporate sector, think tanks, and the educational community itself (Keene and Ladd 1990; Kosters 1990). Sadly, we rarely find educational goals that focus on maximizing opportunities for the development of families and children. The exception is the Head Start program, which in its inception embodied as a critical goal opportunities for parents of low socioeconomic status to attain skills and advance. But significant numbers of African American parents in the lower socioeconomic strata have not attained values, skills, and knowledge that foster competence. Through participation in schools, urban parents can learn new skills and become motivated and determined to grow and continue developing.

Positive and growth-producing environments do not occur by accident. Nurturing educational environments that offer opportunities and challenges for positive growth are created by the concerted efforts of everyone in the system: school administration and staff, families, and children. Political and other social forces, such as state laws, the municipality, and the community, have a critical impact in setting priorities and allocating resources.

As an outcome of their participatory experience in schools, increasing numbers of African American mothers are returning to complete their schooling or to seek advanced training. By so doing, they become models of productive and successful behavior for their children. Evidence suggests that training and education are not only positively correlated with higher income and an increase in the country's knowledge base but with children's successful performance and completion of school. A well-educated work force is key to improving living standards and restoring the country's competitiveness (Kosters 1990).

2
The Participatory Ethos:
An Ideal or Reality?

Participation: A Democratic Ideal

America was founded on the principle of participation, a tradition that directs people to engage actively in organizations and institutions in the wider social system. Particularly appropriate in this context is the working definition of political democracy formulated by Elkins and McKitrick (1954), with its focus on participation in actual decision making by large numbers of citizens whom the decisions will ultimately affect.

Direct participation in communal life and social institutions is integral to democratic society and provides opportunity for lifelong learning. (A more recent conceptualization of democratic theory in the United States emphasizes indirect participation by representation that occurs in the context of elections and group bargaining {Greenberg 1975}). The classical conception of participatory democracy affirms that individuals and their social, political, and economic institutions are in perpetual exchange. Sociologists are concerned with how people engage in and interact with their social environment and in this tradition study formal and informal associations, group affiliations, organizational memberships, and participation in political processes and other social institutions.

Participation as a revered American ideal carries the expectation that large numbers of the citizenry will participate in the affairs of public life with the belief that their contribution is valued and meaningful. The primary function of participation is educational, asserts Pateman (1970). She views education as including psychological development and the expertise individuals gain from carrying out democratic procedures. In *A Nation at Risk*, the National Commission on Excellence in Education refers to the phenomenon of a "learning society" as one committed to value and to create educational systems in which all members continue throughout the life cycle to develop intellectually and emerge better equipped to respond to the social terrain. Participation heightens the capacity of the individual to contribute to and be enriched by society. Lauded as a social good with the prospect of a positive

20

contribution, participation looms basic to a free and growth-producing social order.

The transactional nature of participation is emphasized in this book. My focus is on the reciprocity inherent in the participatory process. At the local school level, participation can be a vehicle for parents to contribute to the wider society. Even the least educated or seemingly unendowed individual has something to offer. The time such a person has to give to an overwhelmed teacher to assist in putting materials away or attending to a distraught child is important. Such participation is simple but meaningful. The contributions of parents participating in schools do not have to be complex to be valued or valuable.

Fundamental to a free society is "the discovery, training and utilization of individual talent. . . . To liberate and perfect the intrinsic powers of every citizen is the central purpose of democracy and its furtherance of individual self realization is the greatest glory" (*Higher Education for American Democracy* 1974:9). John Dewey, the educational philosopher, envisioned democracy as being founded on faith in the potential of human nature—faith in human intelligence and in the power of pooled and cooperative experiences: "It is not belief that these things are complete but that if given a show they will grow and be able to generate progressively the knowledge and wisdom needed to guide collective action" (1927:211). This belief endures as an American value, although vast numbers of Americans remain outside the parameters of participation.

A participatory ethos was a feature of the Selective Service local draft board system. Local citizens were drawn in modest ways into program implementation, primarily by participating in draft board selection processes.

Dimensions of citizen participation have been visible in federal social programming since the 1950s and 1960s in the areas of housing, urban renewal, and delinquency prevention (Mogulof 1973; Ravitch 1974; Morrison 1978). The Economic Opportunity Act of 1964, geared to the needs of the poor, and the underemployed and unemployed, called for the "maximum feasible participation" of the recipients of specified services. These social programs were earmarked for the poor, a disproportionate number of whom were oppressed black and other ethnic minorities. The intent of the legislation was to move the loci of influence and decision making to a level that included the grass-roots citizenry. This politically motivated maneuver, however, ultimately did little to alter in any significant way the economic plight and social dissonance of the targeted population.

The educational sector is a natural setting in which the participatory ethos can unfold and be realized. Historically, this interaction has assumed a number of varying forms in the wake of shifting social, economic, and political forces.

Parents in Education: Changing
Contours and Language

In America's early years, a role for parents in the educational process was acknowledged by virtue of the close relationship between education and the rearing of children. In the 1800s development of parent participation and involvement in public schools occurred in conjunction with the child study and parent education movement. Program initiatives encompassed child study groups, lectures, and circulation of a periodical written expressly for parents. (Berger 1981). Reflected was the belief that both child rearing and formal education share the socialization responsibility that embodies conveying cultural and societal norms, values, knowledge, and skills required for a self-sufficient and productive life.

The institutionalization of the kindergarten in the 1850s marks the articulation of parent involvement in education (Brim 1965). During the ensuing decades, a number of organizations were formed in the United States that focused on the socialization and didactic educational components of child rearing. National organizations—as the Child Study Association, the Free Kindergarten Association, and the National Congress of Mothers, forerunner of the PTA, founded in 1897, among others—targeted the interaction between children and their parents. Emphasized in their parent education programs were child-rearing techniques, parenting skills, nutrition, and other duties related to the role of women as homemakers. For the most part, these programs were geared to middle-class mothers.

The Settlement Houses established between 1870 and 1890 provided social services for the poor, many of whom were immigrants new to American and urban life. Kindergartens located in these Settlement Houses set out to shape these children in accord with mainstream American culture and values. At the same time, they were shaping patterns for parent expectations. Socioeconomic factors, such as race, ethnicity, and income, had a profound effect on the development of child study, parent education, and involvement during this period. Mothers with means affiliated with private associations that represented their view, those with less means were served by Settlement Houses, with their zealous socialization objective.

In 1909, the federal government responded to the poverty engulfing a number of families with the first White House Conference on the Care of Dependent Children. The conference served to heighten awareness of the problems of the poor and was instrumental in the creation of the Children's Bureau three years later. In 1925, the National Council on Parent Education was the catalyst for public funds being allocated for parent education programs designed to reach some of the less privileged. This movement was reinforced by a number of university-established nurseries and preschool programs as adjunct to their research and training, but these programs attracted the middle class. The 1920s saw the growth of the parent education movement as an integral component of many public school preschool programs. The primary mode of disseminating information regarding parenting responsibilities continued to be through lectures, conferences, and literature (Berger 1981).

The positive mood and enthusiasm surrounding child rearing and parent education was muted by the onset of the Great Depression, which changed the lives of many middle-class families and heightened the needs and plight of the poor. An outcome of the White House Conference on Child Health and Protection in 1930 was a recognition of the pivotal role parents play in influencing educational outcomes. A publication released by the Pennsylvania Department of Public Instruction in 1935 asserted that helping parents feel more adequate was as important for public education and societal welfare as was educating children (Berger 1981). Government agencies such as the WPA (Works Progress Administration) sponsored parent education programs for the poor. This high priority given to parent education continued throughout the 1930s and 1940s, well into the early years of World War II. Parent education was linked to and strengthened by the mental health movement of the 1940s, with its emphasis on self-understanding and the understanding of one's children as a requisite for healthy parent-child interaction (Brim 1965).

In the 1950s, the baby boom significantly increased public school enrollments. As active members in PTAs, parents were involved in schools as room parents, fund raisers, and assistants on field trips. At this time, involvement was articulated in terms of instruction being the responsibility of teachers. The parent's duty was to support teachers and schools in carrying out their educational mission. The delineation of involvement as a position in which parents remained in general agreement with school goals, processes, and methods was clearly defined.

The end of the 1940s and the early years of the 1950s were marked by the thousands of Americans who continued to leave rural and small-town America and migrate to central cities in search of employment and opportunities. This phenomenon changed the contours of the classroom in the nation's cities and, ultimately, the interaction between parents and schools.

The 1950s saw increasing emphasis on the social and emotional health of school children. The Office of Education, as part of the Department of Health, Education and Welfare, funded and monitored a number of locally based programs for parents, teachers, and other school specialists. Parent education programs were expanded to include health services and ongoing training of professionals. The success of the former Soviet Union in launching *Sputnik* in 1957 intensified the country's scrutiny of the educational sector and its outcomes.

Changes wrought by the civil rights movement, continuing urbanization, the Vietnam War, and government programming to combat poverty shaped the 1960s and 1970s. Social, behavioral, and educational research demonstrated that a child's development is significantly influenced by the environment. The War on Poverty had as its goal the elimination of poverty and its corrosive effect on large numbers of American children and families. With increasing advocacy at the local community level, the educational sector was affected by sweeping social changes and the reconfiguration of parent participation in education (Davies et al. 1978; Gittell 1978). Those of low socioeconomic status, ethnic minorities, and poor whites were drawn into the day-to-day life of the school as an outcome of government-sponsored educational programming. Head Start, with mandated outreach for parents that included parent education participation on advisory boards and career opportunities, was instrumental. As part of the Follow Through Program, parent participation in the tradition of Head Start accompanied children as they moved on to the first three grades in public school.

In summary, in the late nineteenth and early twentieth centuries, the role of parents in education was articulated in terms of parent education in which parents were the recipient of information and guidance offered external to the functioning of the school. By the mid-twentieth century, the language and form shifted, with the parent's role now being perceived as supporting and reaffirming the teacher's instructional role. Support was in kind, through fund raising and accompanying teachers on field trips. Since the 1970s, the parent role in education has expanded to embrace an active stance in which parents are engaged participants.

Head Start

Head Start, a forerunner in programming and implementing parent involvement in preschool education, has had a dramatic impact on improving American educational outcomes (Berger 1981; Morrison 1978; Schorr 1989; Zigler and Valentine 1979). The most conclusive longitudinal study (Zigler 1985) attests to and demonstrates the ongoing positive educational and social outcomes of Head Start, among them, empowerment of the poor, who develop a commitment to assist and support their children's continuance in the educational system. A vital program initiative includes parents in all aspects of program planning and implementation and in ongoing participation in day-to-day operations of the program. Head Start has proved to be a significant factor in strengthening the psychological development of parent participants and thus the family system.

With a clear mandate to involve parents, the Head Start program has endured for a quarter of a century. While legislation to expand Head Start was approved in the fall of 1992, the funding level provides for only approximately one-third of the nation's needy children.

Participation and Socioeconomic Status

Parent participation as a process varies considerably among schools (Swap 1990). In addition to educational leadership, programming, and incentives, neighborhood, community, and personal variables affect the extent of and degree to which parents become active in their children's school. The popular press and scholarly literature inform us that participation is strongly influenced by socioeconomic factors. Distinct differences can be identified between the participation that occurs in suburban schools, where the population is predominantly white and/or middle or upper class, and that which takes place in inner-city schools located in economically marginal areas, inhabited primarily by African Americans and ethnic minorities.

Parents in suburban communities have a legacy of participation in their children's school, reflected in both active and overt participation in school activities and in support that may be less visible and symbolic. Parental presence in the neighborhood and affluence symbolized by comfortable homes, orderly external environments, and formal associations, such as Little League teams, Jack and Jill, Inc., and the League of Women Voters, send an unambiguous message of the values, norms, and expectations these parents endorse. The values tend to complement those of the teachers and administrators in the local schools. In many instances, these parents may themselves be employed in the educational sector. They are upwardly mobile, eagerly embodying dominant American values. Propelled by their enthusiasm, at times they can become overly involved in the affairs of their children's school, and their participation often experienced as excessive and threatening to school and teacher autonomy. A less seasoned third grade teacher was questioned by an enthusiastic parent about the choice of insect for a science demonstration underway. The parent went on to extol the scientific benefits of an alternative insect. In her eagerness, this occurred in the presence of the class of eight- and nine-year-olds, who erupted into a chorus, chanting their preference for the mother's suggestion. The teacher experienced the episode as degrading and believed her authority undermined. Other teachers have had their grading and efforts to discipline challenged. Such confrontation does little to advance teacher confidence.

In articulating a model of parent involvement in schools when federal endorsement was paramount in the 1970s, Litwak and Meyer (1974) differentiated and delineated the conditions, requisites, and processes pertinent to schools' interaction with parents, noting that they vary in accord with socioeconomic status. They developed a paradigm to identify processes for distancing the interaction between affluent suburban parents and their children's school. This was in contrast to identifying processes to implement parent-school interaction in urban schools.

There is conflicting evidence regarding the relationship of socioeconomic status and parent involvement. Studies demonstrate that while parents in high socioeconomic status communities are involved in their children's school, principals view them as demanding (Goldring 1990). In spite of the perception that these parents will interfere in school affairs and hence the reluctance to engage them, they can be counted on for support and resources. School effectiveness studies reveal mixed findings, noting that some principals of schools with children from low socioeconomic families dissuade involvement, while others encourage parent participation. It is reported, (Goldring 1990), that for those who have attempted involving low-income parents, the outcome has been disappointing, in that those parents were not viewed as being too helpful. The full implication of the difference is complex. However, the contrast suggests that when parents negotiate from a position of economic strength, are assertive, and are prone to intervene in the educational and social environment of the school, their influence is viewed as either sufficient or possibly excessive. For the most part, parental and educational goals in suburban communities are congruent. The parental role of supporting the school program and activities, such as providing leadership in parent-teacher organizations, fund raising, and career day exercises, is compatible with goals articulated in mainstream American society. This participation, an endorsed and anticipated tradition, not only reinforces the academic performance and socialization of children but emerges as a source of additional assets for the school.

Lightfoot (1978) speaks of the success of suburban schools not in terms of their obvious affluence or their being predominantly white but in the consonance between the goals parents have for their children and what teachers view as good educational practice. The dynamic of this interaction reinforces this bond and strengthens and sustains educational goals. A study conducted in 1974 supports the interaction of the role the family plays and socioeconomic factors in influencing the educational process (Morrison 1978).

The idea that those of higher socioeconomic status have a higher degree of participation in the social system is not new. A sociological study conducted in the 1950s in San Francisco reveals that males who lived in more affluent neighborhoods belonged to formal associations, attended meetings, and held offices to a significantly greater extent than a comparable group in a lower socioeconomic neighborhood. Empirical studies examining participation among urban dwellers found that social participation and socioeconomic status have a positive correlation (Kamarovsky 1946; Bell and Force 1956). Yet more recent sociological research reveals a changing pattern. Socioeconomic status remains an even more salient factor in distinguishing joining patterns; however, low socioeconomic status is not necessarily correlated with low participation. London's (1975) work demonstrates reversal of the usual pattern correlating higher income and participation by showing that African Americans in the low socioeconomic stratum who join organizations are more likely to be the most committed participants. Urban schools identified as having successful academic performance and social functioning report that parental representation is a significant factor in obtaining positive outcomes (*Phi Delta Kappan* 1980). Even more recent studies show that racial and ethnic minority parents want to play an active role in their children's education (Chavkin 1989).

The paucity of participation in their children's school by low-income parents living in major metropolitan cities became apparent during the era of the New Frontier and the Great Society. Blacks and other oppressed groups, such as Latinos, increasingly became aware of their powerlessness and the failure of public schools to teach their children basic skills and competencies. They expressed their discontent in a variety of ways, ranging from apathy to boycotts to litigation. They also wanted to have a voice in the way in which the public school carries out its mission in educating their children.

Germain (1979), in exploring the transactional nature of human existence, observes that citizens whose lives are circumscribed by their dependence on society have less of an opportunity to negotiate their circumstances. Their condition insidiously undermines a democratic system and negatively affects the view people hold of themselves and how they are viewed collectively. Two civil rights activists embroiled in the New York City school dispute of the late 1960s, sought to bring adminstrative control to the local level. They demanded that teacher hiring be determined by citizens living in the communities where the schools were located and not by a central office bureaucracy. Powerlessness was declared as a primary factor in causing poverty and they advocated participation as a way to alleviate this debilitating outcome (Ravitch 1974). Those who are denied access and opportunity and function outside the realm of decisions that govern their existence are rendered impotent.

In looking specifically at participation, Parker, Piotrkowski, and Peay (1987) found that participation in Head Start activities had a positive effect on psychological well-being. Mothers who participated more had fewer psychological problems, greater feeling of mastery, and greater life satisfaction. After only one year of program participation, these mothers were less isolated and viewed Head Start as a place to make social contacts. Although the case for a causal relationship cannot be made, it is safe to say that participation in decision making and in learning activities is a critical factor in positive personal outcomes. The Head Start program, with its activities and special programming, was a place of refuge for many mothers and a welcomed alternative to the drabness and lack of challenge in their day-to-day existence.

One of the questions that the studies reported in this book sought to answer was the extent of powerlessness in the lives of the mothers who participated in school programs. They were asked whether they agreed or disagreed with the statement, "There is not much that I can do about most of the important problems that we face today" (Srole 1956). In the evaluation of the Baldwin-King Program in the 1970s, it was found that the intensive program of five years of parent involvement had not changed the pervasive sense of powerlessness of the mothers who had participated. They continued to feel just as powerless as their counterparts in the control school with low participation. On the other hand, their participation did result in significant differences in whether these mothers thought it acceptable to do anything to get ahead (the normlessness component of alienation) and the extent to which life lacked purpose for them (the meaningless component of alienation). (See table A.1 in appendix A). In the 1987 study of the Milwaukee schools, inner-city mothers whose participation was classified as high were twice as likely to reject the idea of powerlessness as mothers whose participation was low (figure 2.1).

Smith (1968) argues that the "absence of power entails general vulnerability and creates dependency. . . . When opportunities are offered without a sharing of power we have paternalism, which undercuts respect, accentuates dependence and breeds a lurking resentment. . . . Power receives respect and guarantees access to opportunity" (p. 313). His treatment of power as absolute control over a person's fate is compatible with powerlessness as explored in this book. Power and its complex properties mitigate the participatory process.

Figure 2.1. Participation and Rejecting Powerlessness

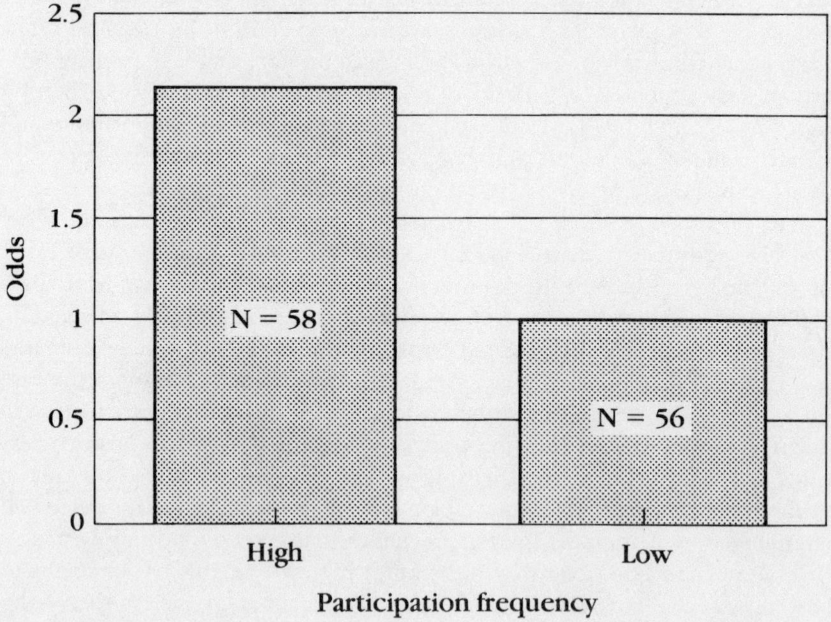

Note: Odds is the log of the ratio of the likelihood that an event will occur to the likelihood that an event will not occur.
Source: Table B.1.

In suburban schools, power issues generally have not surfaced as an explicit cause of concern. It is only when institutions usurp their power or become unresponsive and self-serving that the public exercises its right for a reckoning (Fantini 1974). Due to a myriad of political, social, and economic reasons, most urban schools continue to exclude the very people they serve from meaningful participation, creating a distance that weakens support for and embodiment of dominant societal educational goals. Parents exposed to such situations internalize negative defensive attitudes and assume postures they unwittingly pass on to their children. A cycle of mutual rejection and failure is perpetuated.

Patterns of Participation

Bolstered by the Supreme Court's *Brown v. Board of Education* (1954) decision and the stimuli of the ensuing civil rights momentum, blacks and other minority groups in the 1950s began to express disenchantment with the outcomes of the education of their children. Government-sponsored programs requiring citizen participation paralleled the aspiration articulated by blacks to obtain a "piece of the action" (Mogulof 1973). African Americans raised their voices to express a desire to influence schools as they carried out their mission and, by so doing, frame the course of their children's education (Lightfoot 1978). They became sensitive to inferior education and aware of their own feelings of inadequacy, powerlessness, and alienation in relation to the school (Coleman et al. 1966; Lightfoot 1978; Ravitch 1974; Silverman 1970; Urofsky 1973). This heightened awareness continued into the mid-1970s, accompanied by a range of educational innovative programs designed primarily to meet the needs of the poor, and thus African American children and families. Small in number, these short-lived programs, usually implemented under the auspices of the private and public sector, were not institutionalized. During this period, a few religious and alternative schools established educational programs. The few that have endured, such as Chicago's Westside Preparatory School, continue to target and successfully educate African American children. Urban Catholic schools and some operated by the Black Muslim religious community have had similar successes. Although these schools are important educational institutions, they reach only a small segment of the African American population.

The fervor of that innovative period began to wane by the end of the 1970s. Economic, political, and social forces, reflected in funding deficits, dwindling local and state support, and the lack of a national mandate and leadership, resulted in a downward spiral on the educational front. The outcome affected all children in the nation's public schools. African American students, although they have made gains in academic performance, continue to lag behind their cohort group, and the academic performance of white students remains at a lower level than in previous decades (Keene and Ladd 1990).

The commitment to parent involvement witnessed in the 1970s flounders, a particularly worrisome situation for the nation's poorest and more congested central cities. Even the influential National Commission on Excellence in Education in *A Nation at Risk* acknowledged the role of parents in schools but failed to articulate dimensions of parent participation.

An example of an enduring innovation is the Comer School Development Program, first implemented in the late 1960s in two predominately black inner-city schools in New Haven, Connecticut. A basic premise of the program is the belief that a child's home life and school performance are inextricably related. Hence, troubled schools must form an alliance with parents. Schools in this program undertake an inclusive management approach that brings principals, teachers, professional staff, and parents together, sharing authority. Working as a team, guidance counselors, mental health professionals, and teachers focus on the emotional, social, and psychological needs of individual children. Significant improvement in academic performance and behavior are indicators of the program's ongoing success (Comer 1985; Marriott 1990). Today, this comprehensive initiative, with its viable parent involvement component, is being transmitted to one hundred inner-city school systems across the country (*New York Times* 1990).

It has not been a tradition for African American parents to be involved in such school events as PTA meetings, parent-teacher conferences, and special school programs (Lightfoot 1978). Teachers thus view black parents as apathetic or disinterested. They rarely recognize that these parents' absence or reluctance to take part in school activities is related to their lack of know-how in negotiating the complex bureaucracy of the schools. Neither can the decades of abandonment by the educational sector be dismissed.

Fantini (1974) focuses responsibility for the lack of parent response on the monolithic structure of the school, which continues to be based on a nineteenth-century model incongruent with the needs of a rapidly concluding twentieth century. In the past decade, black parents have become more aware of this dichotomy, expressing their frustration and feelings of intimidation by a school staff that does little to send a welcoming message. In their ambivalence, teachers, principals, and other school personnel fail to develop or utilize strategies that would serve to generate parent involvement (Chavkin 1989). Consequently, African American and other poor parents suffer a dual penalty: a missed opportunity to influence the school in positive and important ways, and experience the gratification that accompanies contribution, and a missed exposure to knowledge and the chance to learn new skills. Both are outcomes of participation that are transferable to other challenging life situations (Alden 1979). For their part, public schools are deprived of the strengths and resources that diverse parents can bring and develop by the efficacy of their participation. Moreover, the schools perpetuate the alienation of African American parents and their children by closing them out of the system in a number of ways.

After more than two decades of contemplation, experimentation, and national discourse, educational determinations such as curriculum, governance, and staff selection remain the preciously guarded terrain of professional educators. Educational decisions are made through administrative hierarchies that rarely include local citizenry (Comer 1980, 1986; Fantini 1974; Fruchter 1984; Heid and Harris 1989; Lightfoot 1978; Lopate et al. 1970). Many principals, teachers, and other school personnel discourage even the less threatening forms of participation such as conferences with minority parents (Chavkin 1989; Johnston and Slotnik 1985). Critics of the educational system maintain that this posture is deliberate, designed to maintain exclusive power. Many school personnel believe that educational decisions and indeed, the educational enterprise itself, rest solely with the professionals. Their intent may not be malicious, but their professional socialization and experiences have failed to prepare them for participation. For others, the power issue is paramount (Jenkins 1981; Morrison 1978). They feel vulnerable by having educational decisions shared or monitored and harbor fears related to job security. The fear is not unreasonable; in the Ocean-Hill Brownsville New York City school dispute, community boards asked to have certain school personnel removed (Ravitch 1974). Yet parent involvement does not have to disintegrate into a face-off between parents and school personnel. With practiced collaboration and consultation, a partnership can be established that is not adversarial.

Participation in decision making and governance, the crux of the matter, can be shared. Professional ownership that militates against parent involvement can be mediated. In an alternative school that after twelve years was subsumed into the Salt Lake City School District, parent participation remains its bedrock. At its inception, a group of parents hired seven teachers to instruct their children. Although the program is now under the auspices of the public school system, parents participate in hiring teachers and in book selection, and they serve on the steering committee, the primary governing body of the school that considers major program policies and issues. Parents in this program provide resources and support in the school and classrooms. They teach specialized lessons (e.g., creative writing, piano lessons) and tutor based on their individual abilities. Even with the mutual commitment of parents and school personnel, this model demands a high level of organization, patience, and flexibility given the variation in parents' skills and availability. "Each teacher must strike a delicate balance between allowing able parents to function independently in creative and effective ways and supporting parents who are less assertive and less confident, so that they grow in their participatory roles" (Johnston and Slotnik 1985:433). This parent-school cooperative sanctioned by the public education sector, even with all of its years of positive outcomes, is no panacea. School personnel are reported to be faced with problems of fragmentation, inconsistent behavior expectations, and attempts at manipulation by students. At times, parents and school personnel disagree vociferously on book purchases. In this upwardly mobile neighborhood, participation is not without demands and drawbacks, but proponents of this program after fourteen years of affiliation note that the benefits far outweigh the burdens (Johnston and Slotnik 1985).

Schools in a number of urban areas that embrace the Comer principles and process "emphasize building relationships based on sharing . . . bring school administrators, staff, teachers, and parents together regularly . . . {and} share authority in managing the school" (Marriott 1990). Academic performance and socialization benefits accrue. A number of inner-city schools using the Comer process report that student behavior and academic performance improved significantly. The League of Schools Reaching Out, encompassing urban elementary schools across the United States, provides support and incentives to increase the participation of parents and to provide a forum in which schools can share experiences as they learn to build partnerships with families and communities (Davies 1990). Individual educational leaders, such as Mary P. Spriggs, principal of the Wilkinson Primary School in Washington, D.C., interrupt the cycle of exclusion by adopting "an attitude of shared decision-making and a sort of shared ownership." With strong conviction, she postulates that people who "know {they} are part of something give it {their} best" (*Washington Post* 1991). The hope is that urban schools will alter and modify the structural arrangements, attitudes, and practices that discourage socially and economically disadvantaged parents from taking an active role in their children's schooling.

Despite federal funding, private incentives, and grass-roots initiatives, urban public school systems, with a few notable exceptions, tenaciously maintain the status quo, failing to program and institutionalize significant interaction with parents. The urban school, often a potpourri of people of different ages, races, socioeconomic statuses, and value orientations, remains elusive and unavailable to its constituency and unresponsive to the ramifications of cultural diversity and socialization demands that have a bearing on cognitive and affective styles. Rising functional illiteracy, low scores on national standardized tests, vandalism, teacher burnout, and parent apathy herald the failure of inner-city schools to fulfill their educational mission.

Cloward and Jones (1963) found that involvement of low-income parents in school activities was positively correlated with parents' evaluation of the importance of education and attitude toward the school as an institution. This is in contrast to Chilman's (1966) finding that the poor are more inclined to anticipate failure and to distrust institutions, including the schools. Continued disregard of this population not only reinforces negative attitudes but fosters low self-esteem and self-defeating behaviors. The cues that children receive from their parents serve to fashion their behavior and sentiments. They experience their parents' feelings of powerlessness and believe that they too have limited or no control over their fate. Accumulating evidence suggests that these feelings of powerlessness and alienation can be abated by social institutions more responsive to the needs of the poor and African Americans (Fruchter 1984; Marriott 1990; Parker, Piotrkowski, and Peay 1987).

There is a relationship between participation as used in this book and social participation or joining patterns in wider society. Systematic data regarding African American participation in wider societal institutions have been accumulating for two decades. In a study examining social participation of African Americans, Lucas (1985) posits, "Because blacks are denied access to various forms of social participation enjoyed by whites, it is argued that they lack basic normative orientations and skills necessary to motivate and enhance their social participation" (p. 98). Such a position is reminiscent of sentiments common among school personnel who want to discourage parent involvement. Variation in styles and types of social participation has been studied, with investigators contrasting ethnic, income, and residential patterns (Martineau 1976). Earlier sociological studies explored the participation of blacks in social institutions and political processes (Babchuck and Thompson 1962; Orum 1966). In conducting a survey in the early 1960s among low socioeconomic status residents in Detroit Orum (1966) found that African Americans were more likely to belong to political and church groups than were their white counterparts, although membership in civic organizations was equal for blacks and whites. Nevertheless, for African Americans, this participation occurred primarily in black associations and organizations rather than in mainstream social and political institutions. Such stratified participation suggests that blacks are trying to compensate for the social exclusion and deprivation that they experience in a racist society (London 1975).

An ethnic community theory suggests that increased race and class consciousness is a precipitating factor for blacks joining organizations (Olsen 1970). Other studies demonstrate that whites are more inclined than blacks to participate in civic, social, and political activities and organizations (Hyman 1971; Janowitz and Marvick 1956). These findings are challenged by the results of studies that demonstrate that when socioeconomic status and education are controlled, participation by blacks is equal to or in some instances exceeds that of whites in a range of social and political organizations (Orum 1970; Olsen 1972; Williams, Babchuk, and Johnson 1973). In using data from the 1970s and controlling for certain demographic variables, Lucas (1985) found no difference between races, both whites and blacks failed to affiliate with political clubs, professional societies, and service groups. A higher percentage of African Americans join action-oriented organizations concerned with political, labor (Lucas, 1985), or civil rights issues or organizations that have a specific focus such as travel, literary, or shared professional interests (London 1975).

Whether participation by low-income blacks is born of compensation or ethnic pride, it is compromised by racism. Proponents of the compensation theory of social participation interpret African American joining patterns as an initiative for seeking ego reinforcement, personal recognition, and prestige that are not forthcoming in a racist society (Lucas 1985). African Americans need to influence the environment. David Bradley poignantly represents this human condition through the simple but penetrating sentiment of Old Jack, in *The Chaneyville Incident* (1981). A black man of limited formal education, Jack insists, "A man has to have a say. . . . Everything a man does that makes any kind of sense, anyways, is on account he wants some say. That's why he builds a fence around his land, an' digs in the ground an' plants in rows; so every time he looks at that piece a ground he'll know, maybe he didn't make it, but he had some say" (p. 41). Bradley speaks in the context of some influence, some power over his lot in life, and how this substantiates a sense of self.

Lightfoot (1978) sees African Americans as waging two battles on the educational front. One, perhaps of a shorter duration comparatively, is a political battle to gain access to dominant school structures. The other, more long term, indeed enduring since slavery, is a psychological battle for education and all its benefits—an educational process that will celebrate and preserve the African American cultural heritage while simultaneously teaching the knowledge, skills, and competencies required for survival in a competitive society. Blacks in the main are still the recipients of poorer quality education than their white counterparts (Kozol 1991; Murphy 1990). Despite the struggle, disenchantment, and disappointment chronicled in historical accounts of the development of African Americans, their faith in American education is unwavering. Although the educational system continues to fail significant numbers of black children, African Americans still believe that education is the most propitious path to the benefits and opportunities associated with upward mobility (Blackwell 1985). Even when the system fails them, the African American community remains available and willing to participate when a genuine opportunity is presented.

Pitfalls and Promises

Arguments for and against in-depth participation by parents in the educational sector abound. Such involvement runs the risk of imposing on parents more responsibility and authority than they can effectively negotiate and manage, and it can lead to role confusion that interferes with the constructive aspects of participation.

This book views disadvantaged parents as significant individuals who bring special skills and knowledge about their culture and community to the school. I do not suggest that the operation of a complex organization like a school be given willy-nilly to unsuspecting and untrained parents who in their zeal and naiveté can demand more than they are equipped to handle. To place parents in a position of having prime responsibility for solving chronic administrative and organizational problems, such as vandalism, truancy, and chronic failure, is inappropriate and would set them up for failure. The typical parent living in a low-income urban area lacks the educational background or experience necessary for making independent curriculum decisions. Nevertheless, the information and know-how these parents can bring to the school is critical to the educational process. They bring information about conditions in their community, their aspirations, expectations, doubts, and uncertainties. As parents question routine school practices, administrators and teachers are challenged to consider implications and alternatives. Parents use their bargaining skills, in assisting school personnel to reach out and engage evasive parents. A group of mothers uses entrepreneurial skills to establish a school-based used-clothes shop. When tutoring, their interpersonal and persuasive skills are used to motivate children to master their lessons. In each instance, the parents' skills and abilities make their mark on the school.

Lightfoot (1978) contends that the African American culture and experience must be embodied in the education of black children as a requisite for maximum educational outcomes. Ravitch (1974) alludes to the risk of including parents in her discussion of community control issues in the New York City school dispute. Although the political and substantive issues in that situation extended beyond parent participation as perceived in this study, her concerns are pertinent. She suggests that the idea of black control of black schools in New York City had a special appeal to diverse groups for their own motives. For example, school administrators were certain that African American parents would fail and then have no one to blame. Powerless parents can, out of their own frustration, inexperience, and ignorance, demand more than they are equipped to handle. The political recourse for those in control of schools may be to "let them hang themselves" rather than negotiating the kind of distribution of power and checks and balances that harness strengths and foster positive contributions.

Parent participation does have drawbacks. The participatory process is time-consuming; conflicts emerge, differences surface, and additional professional time and energy must be directed to implementation and negotiation; power issues erupt and require resolution; and school personnel who believe curriculum and educational decisions are solely within the purview of the professional view parent participation as an encroachment on their territory and resist efforts to program and implement participation (Chavin 1989; Comer 1989; Fruchter 1984; Morrison 1978; Philips 1975; Schraft 1978; Winters and Easton 1983). This negative stance complicates the problem of institutionalizing parent participation.

Empirical small group studies demonstrate that parent participation can have a positive effect on both the organization and the individual. In a replicated classical study, Lewin, Lippett, and White (1939) demonstrated that group members who participate in decision making are more satisfied and enthusiastic about the task and maintain a higher level of productivity than members of authoritarian groups. Participation in the decision-making process serves to validate decisions for participants. Individuals who have taken part in a decision that results in a change that critically affects them are less inclined to oppose the outcomes of change at some future time. Similarly, their participation serves to reduce the prospect that conflict will occur as processes unfold (Bredo and Bredo 1975; Epstein 1991). Within the humanistic psychological paradigm, Greenberg (1978) postulates that involvement in a specified participatory environment can lead to favorable attitudinal and behavioral consequences for the participant individual and improved conditions in the social system.

Social theorist Daniel Fox views citizen participation as having three primary objectives: (1) to decrease alienation, (2) to engage the individual whom society perceives as deviant (outside the mainstream and failing to embody dominant norms and cultural patterns) and (3) to create an organized societal force that provides protection for aggrieved groups and win them a fairer share of the resources (Mogulof 1973). Those in power who embrace dominant societal values do not view society as being alien to the less fortunate in American society. The first two objectives imply a socialization goal, reflecting the psychological impact on the individual and his or her sense of belonging to and place in the wider society. According to Fox, participation is beneficial to society at large in that it serves to perpetuate societal values and norms. This is closely related to the value-added dimension of participation, which refers to the benefit that accrues beyond the explicit and articulated goals—a dimension difficult to measure and document yet alluded to in discussions regarding the positive attributes of participation.

Pateman (1970) speaks of the participatory process as being self-sustaining: "the more the individual citizen participates the better he is able to do so" (p. 24). The benefit of parent participation is sustaining in other ways; it generates the self-confidence and social competence that propels people to seize their environments and utilize resources more advantageously. Habitually apathetic parents discover that their input is desirable and valued. A parent's view of the school becomes more positive, and this attitude can influence their child's academic performance.

Note: Data for the earlier study are analyzed using chi-square analysis and analysis of variance. For the later study, in keeping with developments in social science methodology, the logistic regression model estimates the linear relationship between a dichotomous dependent variable (e.g., powerlessness) and selected qualitative/categorical independent variables (such as participatory status or education). Findings are discussed in terms of the odds for the occurrence of an event. Detailed description of this methodology appears in appendix *B*.

3
Alienation: A View Through Sociocultural Lenses

A number of forces in the social structure can constrain human development. These adverse social and economic forces weigh particularly heavy on the poor who live in America's cities. Increasingly, cities are bereft of adequate housing, safe neighborhoods, challenging employment, primary health care facilities, and effective schools, the minimal requirements to promote human growth and development.

Social and behavioral scientists generally agree that modern life perpetuates alienation. It abounds when social environments neglect citizens' fundamental needs (Etzioni 1968). (The absence of empirical studies exploring alienation in past generations, however, precludes quantitative verification of this assumption {Geyer 1980}.) Large-scale environments characterized by the complexities common to urban life fail to respond to the needs of significant numbers of families and individuals, a particularly compelling conclusion since America's metropolitan areas now claim over 50 percent of the nation's population (U.S. Census 1990).

Contemporary American society is fashioned by rapid social change with increasing industrialization and advanced technology. Deteriorating urban cores with demoralizing social conditions promote maladaptive behavior and other pathologies that affect the wider society, resulting in adaptation problems, especially for ethnic minority groups. A study by Glasgow (1980) of gang life in Los Angeles demonstrated that young black males adopted a life-style designed to compensate for the societal emasculation that they felt.

The Concept of Alienation

A number of disciplines in the social sciences, including sociology, political science, criminology, and cultural anthropology, seek a social explanation of alienation (Geyer 1980). Sociologists line up on either side of alienation as unidimensional, in the Seeman (1956, 1983) tradition, or on the side of alienation as multidimensional (Schacht 1970; Travis 1986). Those who favor the multidimensional formulation argue that each of the different concepts subsumed under alienation—powerlessness, meaninglessness, normlessness, isolation, and self-estrangement—is unique and should be treated as such. Studies that measure alienation as a general syndrome are considered flawed and trivialize the concept (Travis 1986). Conversely, Seeman (1983) reminds us "that the themes that are classically brought under the alienation rubric refer to the fundamental ways in which the individual is related to the social structure" (pp. 171–84).

A number of empirical studies have explored various aspects of alienation as manifested in the social structure. Although Geyer's assertion that the studies have yet to produce a well-integrated theory is shared by many (Lystad 1972; Travis 1986), the concept is sociologically relevant, and its meanings and usage range from the theoretical to the empirical to the popular. Alienation has been examined in the context of the economy, the workplace, the polity, voting patterns, age differences, social class, ethnicity, and patterns of social and leisure group affiliation. Schaff (1980) comments on the role that American sociology and social psychology have played in pioneering and perpetuating the concept of alienation. Perhaps this inquiry is related to the inherent paradox of a tradition of democracy and fundamental human rights coupled with oppression. Seeman, whose examination of alienation spans more than three decades, notes that the popularity of the concept waxes and wanes with the political tide and the fancy of "the cultural intelligentsia" (1983).

Anomie and Alienation

The classical studies that provide the historical context and theoretical foundation for the concept of alienation focus primarily on European males. Marx (1964) and Durkheim (1951) provided critical sociological explanations of alienation, examining it within the context of urban and industrial society. Alienation for Marx and anomie for Durkheim were metaphors for their radical attacks on industrialized society's dominant institutions and values (Horton 1964). Seeking sociological alienation determinants, Marx incorporated alienation as the unifying concept in his economic, social, political, and philosophical formulations linking alienation to causation of social aberrations. Geyer (1980) concurs with Marx that alienation is produced in life when individuals interact with a variety of systems in the macro social environment.

Modernization, industrialization, and urbanization have resulted in a disintegration of the sense of order. Durkheim, in his nineteenth-century study *Suicide*, used the extent to which people deviated from societal norms to operationalize the concept of anomie (1951) "a social situation characterized by a breakdown of a socially accepted system of values and norms of behavior; a situation reflected negatively in the crises of society's regulating influence on the action of individuals" (Schaff 1980:156). Comparable to normlessness, anomie represents a breakdown in societal rules governing behavior. Normlessness refers to the expectation that only unapproved behavior will be successful in bringing about anticipated results (Schaff 1980). Durkheim's primary focus targets compliance, that is, how society maintains order by constraining and keeping citizens in line. In Durkheim's paradigm, an anomic society is one that fosters egotism, meaninglessness, and aimlessness among its members. Self-gratification prevails. Societal cues no longer fashion behavior that is consistent with societal expectations. Cultural constraints are no longer effective. Values are either in conflict or are nonexistent.

Value conflicts and normlessness are not limited to the socially disadvantaged. Corporate and political leaders are committing white-collar crimes. Insider trading, money laundering, and other clandestine financial and political maneuvers blur the line distinguishing ethical dealings. In a society with a large disparity between the haves and the have-nots, when goals are not synchronized with achievement structures endorsed by society, problems arise. Daily, the electronic media display the spoils of a highly technological and consumption-oriented society: a range of luxury items from high-performance cars to precious jewels to trendy sneakers. Rarely is work, the means of acquiring such items, simultaneously depicted.

According to Durkheim, when the economy is no longer restrained by the moral codes of institutions such as the church or state, it dominates self and class interests and breeds anomie among citizens. A social state of normlessness, amorality, and anarchy, anomie can be overcome, according to Durkheim, only by establishing societal rules and adequate social control. Societal members must establish an identification with the system and develop a sense of morality. Certain issues that persist in today's complex society—pro choice versus right to life, for example, and gun control versus the right to bear arms—hover on the margins of societal regulation, elusive to the social control of the less complex societies of Durkheim's time.

Certainly the circumstances existing in the nation's urban centers, characterized by killings of disproportionate numbers of adolescent black males by their peers, bespeak alienating social conditions. Daily newspaper headlines simulate an urban death knell. The turning on one's own is the ultimate end of alienation and despair. Alienation thus emerges as an important concept in analyzing by-products of a disparate existence. "Alienation, in order to make empirical sense, has to reside somewhere in and around the persons who are said to have experienced it" (Erikson 1986:6).

Alienation and the Human Condition

As a form of human adaptation, alienation is particularly debilitating in terms of outcomes for the self and for society at large. Overwhelmed and outdistanced, people protect the remnants of the self by turning away or absenting themselves, consciously or unconsciously, from society. They reject the values and norms of the dominant society that rejects them. When they cannot comprehend the inherent complexities and adverse effects of their daily existence, their abandonment is intensified. Reactions range from benign passivity to acceptance and adherence to societal norms to deliberate disregard for established norms. Some ignore life's trials and avoid interaction with the mainstream. Others engage in marginal or antisocial behavior. Some turn the feelings of desolation inward, blaming themselves. Operating on the fringes of society, their immediate culture and social terrain serve as a protective shield. Alienation emerges as one outcome of an individual's dissatisfaction and disidentification with the social, economic, and political structure of society and may be manifested by five dimensions: powerlessness, normlessness, meaninglessness, social isolation, and self-estrangement (Schaff 1980; Seeman 1959, 1983).

In a comparative study, Middleton (1963) found that blacks were significantly more alienated than whites on all five dimensions of alienation. In contrast, in another study also conducted in the 1960s, Bullough (1967) found that black middle-class suburbanites were less alienated than blacks living in Los Angeles black ghettos. In his analysis, middle-class blacks living in the predominantly white suburbs expressed fewer feelings of alienation, felt less powerless, and scored lower on an anomia scale. Since Bullough's work was undertaken, alienation has been considered a multidimensional concept, yet his study suggests that life in the ghetto fosters a demoralized spirit. Undoubtedly, a number of confounding factors are operating. One is the prevailing political, social, and economic distance in large cities between those who govern and the governed. In contrast, middle-class blacks, like their white socioeconomic counterparts, buy into mainstream political, social, and economic values and attitudes. Unlike disadvantaged urban dwellers, the daily existence of middle-class blacks is not permeated by the dissonance, isolation, and depersonalization associated with inner-city life. A socioeconomic status that supports the basic needs of food, clothing, and shelter and facilitates acquisition of the amenities associated with opportunity and comfortable living militates against alienation.

Another of Bullough's (1967) findings suggests that blacks who are less alienated are more inclined to orient themselves toward mainstream society and not restrict their affiliation solely to black organizations. Their talent and resources, both human and financial, become more available to the benefit of all. Certainly the feeling of being apart from mainstream society is lessened for the privileged, yet even for advantaged blacks, empowerment is compromised by the marginality that defines blacks in America. Bullough's (1967) empirical study, while not conclusive, offers a strong argument that certain social structures and cultural factors perpetuate alienation. A legacy of poverty, limited access to opportunity, marginal education and employment, and urban unemployment perpetuates forms of behavior and folkways that function to reinforce acceptance by one's socioeconomic peers but do not resonate with wider societal norms.

Subsequent scholarly accounts of the 1970s, in response to the perceived deprecation wrought by the Moynihan (1965) report, *The Negro Family* which discussed the relationship between black poverty and family structure, defined marginal behavior as functional in that it perpetuated survival. Wilson (1987), on the other hand, cites the work of that period as a disservice because it reduced scholarly inquiry regarding the etiology of dysfunctional self-defeating behaviors and the relationship to societal structural deficits. By the 1980s, the escalation of "pathology" was quixotic, challenging explanation. Out of the experiences of ghetto life, a bonding and commonality can develop that exceeds usual patterns of social cohesion and results in a lifestyle and interaction mode that are not congruent with that of the larger society. This occurs even though poor urban dwellers, in their daily contact with public institutions, such as schools, are exposed to mainstream behavior and social norms. Subtle differences with the interplay of ethnicity, class, and racism can mitigate against meaningful communication and trigger self-defeating response patterns.

Even in seemingly positive social situations, a school reaching out to the community can evoke alienating behaviors and attitudes. For many, the dissonance with the dominant middle-class society does not go unacknowledged. Further devastating is the disparity between the quality of the lives of poor people and the lives of the more advantaged. The electronic media underscore the entitlement and comfort intrinsic to a life of advantage through news coverage and entertainment programming.

Social alienation occurs when individuals find their social system in conflict with their desires, and they feel estranged from the wider society. Alienation can emanate from sociocultural patterns that are in conflict with basic human needs. The sociological determinants perspective gives limited credence to psychological factors as explanatory variables and maintains instead that alienation is the outcome of deficits in the macro social environment (Geyer 1980). Although social and behavioral scientists distinguish between alienation from society and alienation from self, they acknowledge a close relationship between self-alienation and the social order (Travis 1986). People are defined and molded by their physical and social environment and, in turn, modify and alter the structure of that material and communal world.

African Americans and Alienation in Retrospect

In a sociocultural perspective dating back to slavery, the history of American blacks is that of being relegated to a subhuman status. Keniston (1965) identifies American blacks as victims of "enforced alienation," which has as its root causes psychological outcomes associated with racism and environmental and social deprivation. The lament of the Negro spiritual, "I've been 'buked and I've been scorned," captures and characterizes black expression of alienation (*Hall Johnson Series* 1946). The pathos and poignancy of these words speak to the overwhelming despair that can grow out of alienation.

As a collectivity, blacks suffered primal psychological and social alienation when they were forcibly displaced from their native land, with its supportive cultural and social system. In the New World, black males were denied their traditional role of family leader, protector, and provider and unwillingly resocialized for a dependent, subordinate status in support of the slave culture. Black females were forced to relinquish their maternal role regarding their own progeny as families were dispersed (Winters 1975). "Alienation," says Erikson (1986), "is disconnection, separation—the process by which human beings are cut adrift from their natural mooring in the world as a result of unnatural alien . . . arrangements" (1986:2). The values and primary goals of white American society were not accessible to slaves. Moreover, in support of the slave system, slave holders advanced a general purposelessness among African Americans by eradicating values and the hope that bolster and guide day-to-day existence (Dean 1961). A damning result was the removal of individual and collective dignity.

Ongoing denial of social, political, and economic opportunity since the abolition of slavery has served to perpetuate and foster alienation and impotence among African Americans. After more than three and a half centuries, a disproportionate number of America's black citizenry remain impoverished, undereducated, illiterate, and alienated. In contrast, groups that migrated to this country later (e.g., the Irish and Italians) have become more assimilated in mainstream American culture, establishing a social, economic, and political base yet sustaining their cultural heritage through family, religious, and social institutions. Most European immigrants gained access to the privileges of first-class American citizenship within one or two generations. Non-European Americans have yet to be accepted as full-fledged members of mainstream America.

During World War I, the demand for labor set in motion the great migration of blacks out of the South to pursue employment opportunities available for men and women in northern industry (Terborg-Penn 1978). This period of employment opportunity was short-lived, however, and was followed by the widespread unemployment and subsequent poverty generated by the Great Depression. Blacks in the workplace, with limited skills and no seniority, were the first casualties. The New Deal, with its social and antipoverty initiatives, such as Aid to Dependent Children and unemployment compensation, brought some relief. Following World War II, urbanization and the concomitant renewal of migration of blacks to the cities in search of employment drastically altered the demography and contours of America's central cities. The overall upgrading of and improvement in the economic climate precipitated the relative prosperity of the 1950s. The 1954 Supreme Court decision on school segregation and the 1957 Civil Rights Act became keystone legislation that altered the social terrain. Disadvantaged groups, the majority of whom were black, began to gain visibility. The New Frontier of the early 1960s targeted the abject poverty that coexisted with the affluence that also characterized that period. The War on Poverty, in the mid-1960s, set the stage for a major expansion of community participation and development.

Although the distance between black and white socioeconomic and political accomplishments has diminished, America's cherished goals still remain inaccessible to a majority of black citizens. A study of alienation among black residents in a central Florida city of 18,000 found that alienation was directly related to subordinate racial status and low educational status (Middleton 1963). Racism and educational disadvantage, two major disabling social conditions, block the attainment of American culturally valued goals by a majority of blacks. As a result of the civil rights movement, strides were made in involving African Americans in major economic and political institutions, yet the number included represent only a small percentage of blacks.

In the 1980s and thus far in the 1990s a majority, and therefore disproportionate number, of blacks remain poor, socially dislocated, and powerless. This phenomenon is particularly evident in central cities, where a majority of African American and other racially ethnic minorities live. Forty-five American cities, with a dearth of social and human resources, lay claim to more than half the nation's black population (Rexroat 1990). This pattern parallels the population shift in the nation at large. Poor blacks continue to be neglected in cities as they continue to be victims of under employment, unemployment, de facto residential and educational segregation, substandard housing, and inadequate schools.

The decline of the inner city parallels the shift in the economic structure in America. As a result of the demise of manufacturing in the 1970s, closed plants, and the subsequent dearth of blue-collar employment, worsened by the 1981 and 1990 recessions, cities were no longer able to offer adequate employment, resources, and municipal services. The subsequent exodus of the working class from cities has shifted the balance of urban populations leaving a large number of poor. Poor African Americans suffer particularly. Cultural patterns, stratification systems, and role expectations adversely affect how needs are fulfilled.

Self-Alienation

Acknowledging the popularity of the topic of alienation in psychoanalytical circles, Schaff (1980) stresses that the psychological usage of alienation is a counterpart of the sociological concept, not a substitute. Like Merton, he insists that the inclination to interpret the concept in psychological terms deviates from the original intent. As initially developed by Durkheim, the concept of anomie referred to a condition of relative normlessness in a society or group. Durkheim made it clear that this concept referred to a "property of the social and cultural structure, not to a property of individuals confronting that structure" (Merton 1957:161). The "psychologization" of alienation is not to be minimized. Geyer (1980) refers to the psychological paradigm of internal versus external locus of control that is frequently equated with the powerlessness dimension of alienation. Although it is a psychological construct, Geyer maintains that it is often a better indicator of alienation caused by the macro societal environment than sociological explanations.

Distinguishing between alienation from society and alienation of self continues to engage the interest of social scientists. "Alienation is an attribute of the individual within the context of specified relationships. Alienation is not a free-floating psychic state: it always involves alienation from something." Therefore, it is incumbent on students of alienation to inquire as to what "conditions produce alienation" (Travis 1986:64).

In a comparative content analysis of popular magazine fiction of the 1900s and 1950s, Taviss (1969) suggested that self-alienation is manifested when the individual self loses contact with any desires, even if they are not in agreement with existing social patterns, or when individuals feel incapable of controlling their behavior. In this formulation, societal conditions are blamed for social alienation, while the individual is deemed responsible for the occurrence of the alienation of self. This inclination to dichotomize alienation into self and social causation does not diminish the strong relationship between the two. The interrelationship between self and social alienation is woven into the daily lives of urban dwellers.

Aiesha Jones walks her six year old to within two blocks of Walnut Street School. After watching her daughter cross two streets and enter the school yard, laboriously Aiesha turns and begins her return home. She appears oblivious to the taunting of a group of men crowding the trash-ridden sidewalks. Returning to her one-room apartment in a former motel, Aiesha joins her three-year-old son and thirteen-month-old daughter. The tattered draperies are drawn closed all day, and the television drones on. Aiesha shuns contact with her neighbors and does not respond when the school's parent coordinator makes her rounds in the building. Depressed and despondent, Aiesha has no support from any of her children's fathers and is barely able to eke out an existence from her welfare allowance. Self-alienation is manifested in the helplessness and benign reservation to demoralizing social forces that are experienced by a number of women in Aiesha's circumstances. Their inner resources are few and external challenges pervasive. In interaction with a hostile environment, powerful forces overwhelm the individual self, negating any incentive to face adversity.

The person-in-situation conceptualization in social work posits that humans are in intimate interaction and transaction with their environment. Environments play a critical role in shaping the individual, as do citizens in shaping environments; neither is easily separated from the other. Often proponents of the self versus social causation of alienation fail to focus on the critical point of intercept. "Effective behavior requires a 'goodness of fit' between personal abilities and environmental demands and supports . . . which strongly influences adaptation and competence" (Maluccio 1981:8–9). Regardless of where causation is located, alienation occurs within an environmental context. Antecedents of alienation cannot rest solely on the individual who brings genetic, cognitive, and behavioral factors to the process of interaction. Human deviations from societal norms are related to social conditioning and are not biologically determined (with the exception of individuals with organic brain dysfunction) (Merton 1968). In a comprehensive construction, self-alienation emanates from an individual's alienation from society, and its institutions and citizens, and the configuration of the individual's own ego structure (Schaff 1980). This alienation of self is reactive to a society that has a definitive role in the alienating process.

Dimensions of Alienation

Alienation as a popular research theme and explanation of disconcerting social phenomenon has endured for the past three or four decades (Schaff 1980; Seeman 1983). Numerous empirical studies focus on delineating a unidimensional concept and exploring the relationship between the alienated individual and the social order. Other studies explore the varying dimensions of alienation. Underlying the concept of alienation is the assumption that individuals in all societies have a fundamental need to belong, to be a part of, to be accepted. Individuals seek affection, recognition, and satisfaction and obtain their identity from both primary (family) and secondary (peer) groups. Group life and acceptance by the group looms critical. This process is complicated for blacks as they simultaneously seek acceptance by the dominant white group and their referent group. The process is wrought with ambiguities, as complete acceptance by the majority population is not forthcoming. Rejection, with its concomitant feelings of anger and remorse, results.

In earlier groundbreaking work, Seeman (1959) specified five components of a unidimensional alienation. Later he averted the unidimensional-discrete debate, focusing on further delineating the attributes of four components of the alienation theme—powerlessness, meaninglessness, social isolation, and self-estrangement—and reaffirming the usefulness of the concept in evaluating the individual's relation to society (Seeman 1983).

Powerlessness

The alienation variant most frequently referred to in contemporary professional literature and popular accounts, *powerlessness* refers to alienation in a sociopsychological sense. It includes external isolation from the larger community and internal isolation characterized by low self-esteem and withdrawal. Of all the components of alienation, the most devastating is the feeling of a lack of power. Powerlessness connotes "the degree to which man feels powerless to achieve the role he has determined to be rightfully his in specific situations" (Clark 1959). Powerlessness is a killer of dreams for everyone. Seeman (1959) defines powerlessness as "the expectancy or probability held by the individual that his behavior can not determine the occurrence of the outcomes, or reinforcement he seeks." This conceptualization refers to expectancies regarding influence or control over the social, economic, and political order. It is not an index of personality adjustment, but it will influence the personality and self-esteem.

Powerlessness is not constant across varying social situations. When individuals move from one social sphere to the other, powerlessness can be mediated. Consider the case of Tanya Harvey, an attorney and single mother of seven-year-old Malcolm, who is experiencing some difficulty in school. At a parent-school event, Ms. Harvey interprets as a criticism of her the teacher's comment that she is unable to give Malcolm the attention he needs in school, given the number of children in her class. Somewhat condescendingly, Ms. Harvey points to other parents, many of them less advantaged, who are having difficulty in controlling their children. She remarks that the teacher cannot respond to her son's needs, since these other children whose behavior is dysfunctional require an excessive amount of her time. In her outpouring, she adds that neither do their parents have the responsibility of a demanding job. Momentarily, she loses her composure in the wake of experienced powerlessness. When she leaves the school situation and returns to her job, she will regain some semblance of power that emanates from her position in a prestigious law firm. The poor mothers in this social scene have no such remedy; no oasis of power awaits them. The powerlessness of their existence permeates all of their social interactions. The powerless theme resounds among the socially dislocated.

A number of empirical studies conducted in the 1960s explored varying dimensions of alienation among blacks. Willie (1968) demonstrated that when compared to their white urban counterparts, urban blacks experienced a heightened sense of powerlessness. Geyer (1980) viewed powerlessness as an outcome when the choices of action available to an individual are diminished. In public schools, special education deliberations and outcomes provide a cogent example. Public Law 94–142 mandates informed consent, a form of parent participation, in special education considerations. Although due process is clearly stipulated, at times the process as carried out at the local level fails to engage and empower parents. Such was the situation involving Kareem Jacquoo and his wife, who were summoned (in their perception) to an educational planning conference at their nine-year-old son's school. They had been informed of Kwame's persistently disruptive behavior, poor academic performance, short attention span, fighting, and physically threatening his teacher. At the planning conference, they were outnumbered by the presence of five school personnel. The parents were overpowered not only by numbers but by the authority vested in each school representative by virtue of professional affiliation. When informed of the outcome of the personality and educational assessments and the recommendations, initially Mr. Jacquoo balked, but he acquiesced when confronted with the alternatives, lamenting, in despair and helplessness, "We're at your mercy."

In a special education system that includes a disproportionate number of African American, poor, and minority children, parents approach the process with distrust and fear. Often, insufficient time is given to the process of engaging parents, which can be lengthy and absorb what appears to be an inordinate amount of scarce professional time. Most of these parents cannot process the data and concentrate on the extent and range of implications contained in home studies, educational assessment including psychological, and in some instances, psychiatric findings. As a result, the focus is lost, diminishing the expectation of positive outcomes. Procedural changes at the local level could modify factors that exacerbate the distance between parents and the school. However, wider systemic changes are required to alter the outcome of desperation and powerlessness these parents experience.

Powerlessness pertains when any behavior that the individual decides upon fails to bring about the goal sought. Mary Largo and her three children are homeless. For over a year, she has been thwarted in her attempts to find affordable housing. Each month the family must move from one shelter to another, a shattering experience for the children, who rarely attend the same school more than three to four weeks at a time. Due to their erratic attendance, Ms. Largo is constantly sought after by attendance personnel. Given the totality of her experiences, she suffers the desolation and defeat of powerlessness.

The interaction occurring between the individual and social forces in the wider system is critical to understanding powerlessness. Geyer (1980) connects powerlessness as an output to behaviors that are self-defeating—behaviors that one is unable to unlearn, due primarily but not solely to limitations in the social system. This interplay is evident in a health care system where prenatal care is available but sustained encouragement, guidance, and skilled outreach scarce. Pregnant teenagers fail to utilize the service and, upon questioning, cite their fear of the pelvic examination (Schorr 1989). With targeted health care programming, these girls are capable of learning and adopting behaviors that not only ameliorate the immediate situation but are transferable to other life challenges. The paucity of positive inputs from society in alienation-inducing situations exacerbates negative interaction and the accompanying impotency. Extension of Geyer's conceptualization advances the idea that the powerless individual is neither exposed to nor convinced of the necessity of learning alternate behaviors, and thus the potential for growth is stunted. When poor inner-city parents repeatedly break appointments with school personnel and human service agencies and become regarded as sullen and noncommunicative, they adopt the behaviors of the uninfluential. Eventually this passivity gets internalized; when questioned about a reoccurring problem, many will shrug their shoulder, indicating, "whatever . . . " or "I don't know," when in actuality they do know. Their initiative has been surrendered. Consequently life continues to be overwhelming and untenable, perpetuating powerlessness.

Seemingly hopeless conditions do not have to be readily accepted. Professionals in the inner city can be catalytic. A principal of a large high school in a northeastern urban city relates the following story. His district was concerned about the increasingly large numbers of pregnant girls who dropped out of high school, although a comprehensive program geared to their special needs was offered in the school. The situation had persisted over a period of time, when it was decided to contact and survey the dropouts. To everyone's surprise, the primary cause for their nonparticipation was simple: the clothes the girls customarily wore, jeans or leggings, were too tight and as their pregnancy advanced no longer fit; having nothing to wear, they stayed at home. When the school volunteers started a maternity clothes bank, many students returned to the program, and the numbers graduating increased dramatically. What is tragic is that not one of the dropouts had come forward or approached a sensitive and available professional or support staff about their plight. It was only following interaction between a volunteer and a student that the issue of inadequate clothing surfaced in casual dialogue. These adolescents appear to have inherited the resignation of the powerless.

The powerless believe that one's behavior cannot affect outcomes or result in what one desires. "Why even try?" turns into, "Why even show up for the appointment?" In dialogue subsequent to completing the questionnaire used in the study for this book, one mother passionately rejected the idea that she was "helpless" and "couldn't do something about problems important to me." The context in which *important* is defined is key. For this woman, important problems were those that had a direct effect on her and her family. She did not negate national problems, but they were not the focus of her attention. Rather, she identified problems that impinged directly on her survival.

Mothers who take part in school activities express fewer feelings of powerlessness than their low-participant counterparts.

Meaninglessness

Meaninglessness refers to an individual's sense of understanding the events in which he or she is engaged. If the social situation is so unclear and muddled that the individual does not know what views to hold, confusion and ultimately avoidance occur.

Respondents in studies of meaninglessness are questioned about their expectations—that is, the extent to which they can anticipate and weigh outcomes. What is sought is evidence as to whether an individual can foresee satisfactorily the result of stated objectives and planned actions (Seeman 1959).

Numerous parents in disadvantaged urban communities, an overwhelming number of them unmarried black mothers, are characterized by meaninglessness. Mainstream society expects that all Americans will embody primary American values and goals such as self-sufficiency, initiative, and independence. But for a combination of complex social, economic, and personal reasons, this outcome fails to materialize for many. And as Wilson (1987) reminds us, third generations of impoverished black families, of which over 50 percent are headed by women, inherit the downtrodden mentality that accompanies poverty. This translates into a passivity that has a negative effect on confidence in oneself and one's capacities and adversely affects the belief in and commitment to education.

Most American parents continue to believe in the potential outcomes of public education, although there is nationwide concern about the efficacy of educational outcomes. Parents anticipate that after twelve to thirteen years in the public school system, their children will accumulate certain knowledge and skills and develop certain values. It is expected that the educational process culminating in high school graduation will prepare their children for responsibility in the workplace or for undertaking postsecondary educational training or study.

In 1989, 43 percent of adult Americans expressed dissatisfaction with the performance of the educational sector, reflecting a 15 percent decrease in support since 1973. Yet this same population remains committed to education, with almost 70 percent indicating willingness to pay higher taxes for improving public education. Some educational analysts, however, maintain that a lack of resources is not the source of the problem with public education (Keene and Ladd 1990). Parents readily acknowledge the discontinuity between their expectations and their actual experience with outcomes. The incoherence and the bewildering relationship between ongoing support and dissatisfaction is representative of Seeman's formulation of meaninglessness. In today's world, for the majority of poor urban parents, the reality belies this expectation. They feel profoundly betrayed.

Historically, blacks have viewed education as a means out of economic dependency and powerlessness. Although the number of blacks completing high school continues to rise, reaching nearly 82 percent in 1989 for those between the ages of twenty-five and twenty-nine (U.S. Bureau of the Census 1990), large numbers of African American young people continue to graduate from public schools deficient in basic skills and knowledge. Undereducated, they are unprepared for the demands of a highly technological workplace and find little gratification in the service-related employment awaiting them.

Almost half—52 of 114—of the mothers in the 1987 study reported in this book neither graduated from high school nor held a high school equivalency certificate. Less than 40 percent (39 women) held a high school or general education diploma. The number of mothers lacking high school credentials in the age group considered in this study exceeds national norms. The National Center for Education Statistics (1990) defines the high school completion rate among African Americans, by diploma or equivalency, as 83 percent based on eighteen- or nineteen-year-old youth not enrolled in secondary or grade school. Although there is some debate as to the basis of calculation, dropout rate statistics indicate that the percentage of those with high school credentials increases as age increases. None of the 114 mothers in the study was under twenty. Slightly more than half were between ages twenty and twenty-nine. In the course of examining the interaction of participation status in school and education level—that is, whether one is a high- or low-frequency participant in school-based activities—education surfaces as the primary factor in whether a mother rejects the idea that she is unable to absorb and process information about the world (figure 3.1).

Although the education level of this population may be atypical, the findings regarding the relationship of education and alienation are in keeping with those of other studies. Too many disadvantaged African Americans appear to have relinquished the viability and potential of education. Their impoverished reality has enslaved their spirit, confirming the denial of their dreams. Uncertainty, confusion, and aimlessness characterize their unsatisfactory lives. Alienation occurs when the individual is uncertain as to what to believe and flounders in the abyss of indecisiveness.

Normlessness

The third component of alienation encompasses the expectation that illegitimate means have to be used in order to realize culturally prescribed goals (Merton 1968; Seeman 1959). As guidelines for action, norms chart the course for changing desires stimulated by society into actions or acquisitions (Geyer 1980). Seeman, in conceptualizing normlessness, recognized that inputs, such as resources, access, and opportunities from certain parts of the environment, are at odds with outputs—both the intrinsic and concrete re-

Figure 3.1. Education and Rejecting Meaninglessness

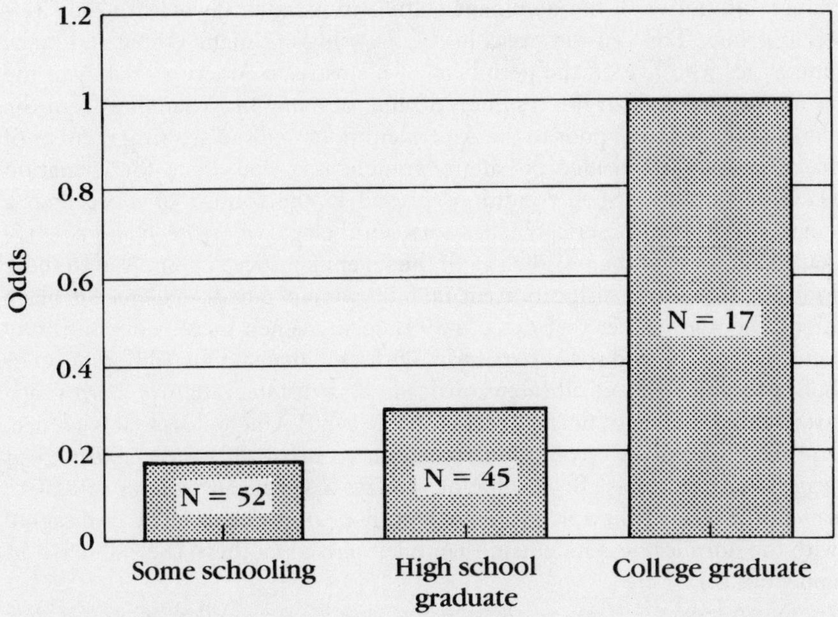

Note: Odds is the log of the ratio of the likelihood that an event will occur to the likelihood that an event will not occur.

Source: Table B.2.

wards. As a result, the decision to seek goals may require using means that the dominant society defines as undesirable or illegal.

The popular and mass media emphasis on materialism and accumulating acquisitions awakens yearnings that are frustrated for many Americans because of restricted means and access. Disproportionate numbers of black children are being murdered for sneakers and leather jackets or because of petty jealousies. The discontinuity between possessions as a desirable good and a legitimate means for attainment is perpetuated. The high conspicuous consumption prevalent in the inner cities, particularly among those engaged in drug dealing and prostitution, sends conflicting messages to youth, including those who embrace sanctioned American values. When certain success goals are depicted so widely, with no emphasis on institutional means that ensure access and opportunity, thousands of poor families, children, the elderly, the unemployed, and the homeless are excluded from the benefits of opportunity and success. Consequently, culturally prescribed goals are at odds with the dominant societal goals.

Norms are predicated on and emanate from the will and behavior of the society. An individual's identity is sanctioned and sustained by acceptance and approval of a particular referent group. In order to succeed and maintain approval and acceptance, one is expected to adhere to certain values and norms. In some instances, subcultural group members may have to violate the values and norms of the dominant culture to maintain favor with their referent group. This tension exists in the daily lives of many ethnic and racial minorities who live on the periphery of mainstream America. A shift in the economic order, with the resultant decline of many black families from the ranks of the working poor to the dependent poor and the growing number of black households headed by single women, is a ripe arena for alienation (DeFrancis 1991). Such conditions prevail in the context of more than a quarter of African American males between the ages of eighteen and twenty-four falling within the jurisdiction of the juvenile justice system. Add to these indicators of social dislocation an unemployment rate among recent black high school graduates that exceeds 39 percent. When there is discontinuity between cultural and social structures, with each demanding a different set of behavior and attitudes, the tension leads to a disintegration of norms, approximating a state of normlessness (Schaff 1980). Unemployment, violence, and drug trafficking—conditions common to urban life—are indicators of general normlessness. Being employed plays a significant role in refusal to sanction deviant behavior. Employed mothers are twice as likely to disagree with the normlessness statement than unemployed mothers. (See table B.3 in appendix B.)

Normlessness is not peculiar to a particular social class but transcends economic strata, as demonstrated in the shady dealings in the savings and loan industry, hostile take-overs, and the blatant criminal activities of some corporate executives. Alienating conditions prevail in view of the means individuals use to attain goals. In such a political and economic climate, it is not surprising that there may be a high expectancy among citizens that socially unapproved behaviors are required to achieve certain goals.

Such diametric situations breed anomie or normlessness. In these circumstances, the most effective means for goal attainment, legitimate or not, can become preferable to institutionally prescribed and endorsed conduct.

Social Isolation

Another component of alienation, social isolation refers to the individual's internalizing an alien feeling in respect to society and its culture. When one is isolated, a breakdown of interaction with the environment is evidenced. Within the configuration of isolation, there is inhibition and inactivity rather than activity. Focusing on sociological determinants, Geyer (1980) offers an environmental explanation for social isolation as limitations that are due to the immediate social, economic, and political order.

Slavery, Jim Crow laws, discriminatory practices, and abiding racism have sociologically imprinted the psyche of African Americans. A legacy of subjugation breeds a potential for attitudes and behavior reflecting social isolation. Repeated defeat and denied dreams reinforce these attitudes and begin to erode motivation. Ongoing denial and manipulation of access and opportunity moderate individual and collective achievement so that no longer is the goal in harmony with the objectives of the body politic. Resignation to social and economic inequities becomes acceptable as the weakened and vulnerable barely muster strength to meet their daily needs of food, clothing, and shelter. The homeless who wander the streets of central cities epitomize the disconnectedness associated with isolation and alienation. At times, even the more enfranchised retreat to the protectedness of uninvolvement.

Increasing numbers of inner-city black families are shut out of mainstream America by virtue of generations of poverty buttressed by a perceived lack of sharing in basic American values. Language patterns and cultural differences foster isolation. Individuals do not come to value the goals or beliefs that are typically valued in the larger society.

The passivity and benign resignation that is observed among many poor black mothers is characteristic of outcomes borne of social isolation. Generally they avoid contact with the school. When contact is unavoidable, they present as indifferent, socially limited, psychologically distant, beaten, or embattled. Keenly aware of the authority vested in school personnel, they often resume a retreatist posture. The very people who feel deprived by the existing social order are victimized by the disparities (Geyer 1980).

In Geyer's paradigm this sociologically determined alienation is the outcome of interaction with wider societal structures. Isolation results from the interaction of the self with a social order characterized by a lack of jobs, schools without resources, substandard housing, and inadequate medical care. As a disadvantaged collectivity, the poor have neither the resources nor the will to do battle with the debilitating societal forces. Traditional and contemporary sociological thought concurs with Thibault (1981) that those who experience alienation are deprived of the means necessary to eradicate or oppose it. Isolation stems from a void in supportive interpersonal interaction and exclusion from the norms or values or culture of one's society (Geyer 1980).

In his seminal work *The Truly Disadvantaged* (1987), Wilson integrates isolation and self-estrangement as the degree of social isolation, "defined as the lack of constant or of sustained interaction with individuals and institutions that represent mainstream society." He decries the barren and polluting ghetto neighborhoods, devoid of model citizens whose daily lives and behavior sanction dominant societal values and goals. The disadvantaged are "socially isolated from mainstream patterns of behavior" (p. 60). They internalize self-deprecating attitudes and engage in self-defeating behavior.

Self-Estrangement

The isolation that comes of negative social and economic forces translates for many into self-estrangement, a complex concept that tends to overlap with the other components of alienation (Merton 1968; Schaff, 1980; Seeman 1959).

Both psychiatry and psychoanalysis seek to explain self-estrangement. Overwhelmed by the effort required to negotiate a deficit-laden environment and constant deprivation, an individual protects himself or herself by relegating painful experiences to the recesses of the mind (Geyer 1980). Alienation in this context refers to a state of being in which the person finds the self foreign. There is a disconnectedness—in essence, a separation from self. The self is defined and reaffirmed in terms of interaction with those outside the self. When estrangement occurs, social exchange and interaction with society become curtailed (Schaff 1980). As individuals internalize negative outcomes, their personal histories become distorted, and they sink further within themselves, with diminishing interaction with the environment. Noting that self-estrangement takes place more or less on an unconscious level, Geyer suggests that isolation is the outcome when the individual discards or inadvertently relinquishes life goals. Or it may occur because expectations are thought to be beyond reach or to attain them would exact a higher personal cost than the individual is willing to yield (Geyer 1980).

Although treated separately in the literature, self-estrangement and meaninglessness are conceptually close and in some aspects overlap. Meaninglessness suggests a lack of conscious engagement in the quest for understanding. When understanding is not forthcoming, disengagement occurs. Self-estrangement connotes disconnectedness in which engagement fails to materialize. An outcome of detachment is common to both dimensions. Disintegration occurs both within the individual and between the individual and the social environment. Self-estrangement refers primarily to the inability of the individual to find and become engaged in rewarding activities. An example is those dropouts who, after years of inattentiveness, chronic truancy, failure, or marginal school performance, claim the curriculum is not relevant to their needs. School attendance holds no promise for them; they tune out. No longer are they connected to the articulated rewards of education. The outcome is devastating. Those with marginal or nonexistent skills, including many high school graduates, enter a high-technology postindustrial society functionally illiterate, disillusioned, and without purpose. They are ripe targets for the illicit activities rampant in urban conclaves.

Alienation emerges as self-dissatisfaction and disappointment with certain structural elements of society. Originating in the interaction between self and society, alienation is the outcome of disunity between societal demands and values, and individual needs.

Alienation and African American Women

For black women, racism and sexism negatively affect the development of the competence that comes of productive experiences. This process for African

American women is wrought with complexities as they struggle to negotiate three distinctly troubling but overlapping dimensions: the damaging social, psychological, and economic outcomes that affect African Americans regardless of gender; the increasingly devastating outcome of black male development as the end of the twentieth century nears; and the implication for black women's development as they strive to define their own voice as empowered and competent citizens.

Toni Morrison's characterization of Jadine in *Tar Baby* depicts the ambivalence and soul-wrenching choices confronted by a black woman in establishing a separate and integrated competent self. If Jadine, a young African American woman socialized in the aftermath of the civil rights movement and educated in Europe, acknowledges her identity as molded by her psychosocial experiences, she denies the essence of her being that is intimately entrenched in the narrative of blacks. The narrative is caustic with the lessons of denied opportunity, denigration, poverty, and powerlessness. It is Jadine's own socialization that influences her preference for a life deliberately separate from her history. Yet she remains tormented by the guilt that is a by-product of her denial. The issues of race and gender are intertwined in her story (Mobley 1987).

In the early and mid-nineteenth century as freed black men formed their own antislavery organizations, they debated whether women should take part in the fight against slavery and whether women should be educated. The importance of education did not elude the freed men who, having achieved empowerment by their own literacy, endorsed education for black women. During the same period, white leaders of the women's rights movement resisted establishing equitable participation in it by black women. Thus, given their shared exclusion and oppression due to race, African American men and women formed alliances. Both "were expected to gain meaningful education and to exercise their moral obligation to uplift the race and the society" (Terborg-Penn 1978:31). For the most part, this egalitarian spirit was evident at the turn of the century. Part of the message was that African Americans fortunate enough to be educated were morally bound to assume responsibility to alleviate societal ills affecting the less fortunate majority of blacks. The participation of educated African American women in meeting this challenge was evident in their teaching and social service as they began to develop their own voice.

In the first quarter of the twentieth century, black women's participation was largely shaped by their male counterparts, which was in turn shaped by the societal imperatives of discrimination and racial subjugation. In the South, African American women were successful particularly in mounting social programs for poor and destitute blacks and forging ways to advance their own education. The legacy of participation by educated African American women has expanded over the decades into the public and private sectors, corporate board rooms, the military establishment, and local, state and national politics.

Yet a majority of African American women are not within the ranks of those empowered. These are the mothers who live in poverty and are responsible for the upbringing of over 40 percent of the nation's African American children. Often they are destitute, depressed, and overwhelmed by their desolate existence in America's unnurturing cities. It is this population with whom the school must interact, engaging and motivating them to share in and support educational goals.

Schools across the country find this population exceedingly difficult to engage. It is not that each does not try, but they become engulfed in the chasm of disparate life experiences that are largely associated with survival issues. As an example, a seventy-year-old grandmother and her older sister have responsibility for nine-year-old James, whose mother died of a drug overdose when he was five. Based on rigorous entrance requirements, James has been selected to attend a school for the gifted, located in a distant affluent neighborhood. Puzzled, the two women are uncertain as to whether this is the "right thing" for James. "Those are rich folks over there." Given their misgivings and uncertainty, they become silent, bewildered, and frustrated. The school principal cannot understand their reluctance: "James is the first student from Caine School to be accepted for the program." His guardians cannot envision a role for him in a society that has rejected them. In turn, the principal finds it incredulous that these two women do not "jump at the chance of a lifetime" for the child. James thus recieves confused signals. Previously happy and excited by the attention he received at school upon notification of his acceptance, his elation is modified by the uncertainty as to whether it is really something good if it makes his granny sad. Although James says he wants to go, his grandmother maintains she and her sister know what is best and decline the offer. Overwhelmed with the experiences of urban living, this opportunity becomes another terrain they cannot negotiate. Alienated and isolated, they remain estranged from the goals that schools embody and the values and norms that schools embrace.

The remedy for alienation lies in equalizing opportunity and access to resources. On a more intimate level, alienation can be lessened by making information available and extending access to social system controls. Participatory processes that occur in schools as a microcosm of society offer an arena for adjusting the damaging outcomes of alienation.

4

Comparing Participation in School Activities: The Parent-School Activity Index

P arent involvement is invaluable in terms of the promising relationship that can develop between school personnel and parents, the untapped resources of parental talent that can be brought into schools and the favorable educational community that is a by-product of this interaction. Of major importance in activating parent participation in educational activities is the idea of ownership. Participation presupposes a sharing of information, access, accountability, and the power inherent in making things happen. Ownership implies an exclusionary relationship that is less open and less sharing.

Ownership and Inclusion

In the 1960s and 1970s, the issue of ownership permeated considerations of the role of parents in their children's education. But since that time, this vocal activism has subsided. Today, with few exceptions, inner-city parents appear more reticent regarding issues pertaining to their involvement. Given the pervasive problems of poverty, drug-related violence, and unemployment, the energy of families residing in inner cities is exhausted in the daily struggle for survival. They lack determination and energy for tackling a seemingly distant and unwelcoming school bureaucracy, and there is little help from national and state-sponsored educational programs, which in the 1970s had offered hope for a sustaining partnership. The repressed stance of disadvantaged parents seems to be a result of their perception of how they believe school personnel view their role as partners in the educative process.

The perception of educational ownership that parents experience as excluding them can be heard in their voices. Minority parents report that they "were intimidated by the staff and institutional structure of the schools and that often they felt awkward about approaching school personnel" (Chavkin

1989:120). More than 1,000 teachers and 2,000 public school parents participated in the Metropolitan Life Survey of the American Teacher, which revealed these sentiments. Their perceptions are accurate. They are not undiscerning of the hesitancy of educators "to involve parents actively in the on-site educational process" (Heid and Harris 1989:29). In such a climate, welcoming behaviors on the part of school personnel can be puzzling. In 1985 at the Dawson School in Milwaukee, a group of parents expressed disbelief upon arriving at a meeting one hour late to discover that administrators, teachers, and school social workers had awaited their arrival before starting the meeting. In addition to conveying to parents the value of their contributions, this action on the part of school personnel reinforced a sense of worth within the parents.

In spite of positive outcomes in a number of enduring programs throughout the country, most school staff remain reluctant to engage parents in responsible school-based collaborative efforts in which planning and/or decision making is shared (Zeldin 1990). This reluctance can be understood given the dearth of positive examples of parent participants and the absence of state directives and policies designed to govern parent involvement in education. Without state or municipal guidelines or policy, the onus falls on individual schools and teachers to develop their own programs. Some school staff, out of their own commitment to engage parents in meaningful day-to-day school experiences, struggle on their own to implement what is considered a very complex process. For the most part, without systemic support these endeavors by well-meaning teaching professionals are doomed to fail. In some cases, the negative outcomes reinforce the ambivalence that resists participation, inadvertently giving credence to the parents' perception of exclusion.

The invitation to participate implies that one's ideas are valued and that one is worthy of being included in a particular social system, thus satisfying a basic human need to belong and to be accepted. Beckoning one to share in is perceived as positive. The act of being invited to become part of a dynamic interaction conveys the belief that the recipient is capable of sharing in the direction and activities of the collectivity. It is assumed that as an outcome of their participation and socialization, the newly initiated will take on the aims and values of the group. When disadvantaged parents are not encouraged to become involved in school activities or events, they perceive schools as discouraging their input, and they retreat from what is experienced as intimidation and rejection (Chavkin 1989; Zeldin 1990).

Occupying the position of power, schools have a responsibility to extend invitations to parents and to convey the message that their involvement is desirable. Accompanying any such initiative must be the endorsement and implementation of processes that govern and make participation viable. All programs must have a purposeful and deliberate vision, a professional position with dedicated responsibility for implementing participation, and a full-time community liaison.

The Practicality of Participation

Participation in the context of the school is not an elusive concept but is characterized by specific functions and results. It presumes a connectedness to educational goals and objectives and presupposes the knowledge, skills, and abilities to carry out tasks (or, if requisite competencies are not apparent, the capacity or potential to develop). Activities are conduits for developing competence. In task-oriented situations, such as those considered in this book, productivity and accomplishment are anticipated outcomes.

The lives of a large number of inner-city women are barren, subsumed in the day-to-day drudgery of struggling to make ends meet for their children and themselves. When these women receive an invitation to come to school and assist, a positive message is conveyed regarding their capacities. This in itself becomes a motivating factor.

A group of mothers who had been active in the Parent Center at the Ellis Elementary School in Roxbury, Boston's inner-city district, organized a special "fathers' breakfast" to acknowledge the role and concern of inner-city males in the responsibility of raising children (Johnson 1990). Participation in this activity by disadvantaged mothers, most of them African Americans, grew out of a number of positive experiences in the Parent Center. Experiences that cultivated their own sense of well-being culminated in their staging an activity to counteract the negative images surrounding inner-city black males. The school endorsed the idea of the breakfasts as a vehicle to convey information about "school curriculum and activities and to promote parent-teacher dialogue" (Johnson 1990). The interaction that accompanies such initiatives is beneficial to schools, staff, parents, children, and, ultimately, society at large. Involvement in a range of activities can serve to strengthen the bond and understanding between school personnel and parents. Shared participation functions to reduce barriers.

Involvement in on-site day-to-day educational activities is basic to the perspective presented in this book. However, one must not lose sight of the importance of parents as educators in their own homes. Even parents with minimal formal education or who live in marginal circumstances can support their children's studies by supervising homework, visiting public libraries, and inquiring each day about what took place in school. Bogart and Le Tendre (1991) speak of homeless families who take their children to community-based tutorial and homework centers. Positive interaction with school personnel can result in parents' appreciating and valuing education and conveying this sentiment to their children in spite of economic limitations.

School Activity and Self-Esteem

Participation in schools serves as a conduit for personal development. Many poor mothers have not had opportunities to be visibly productive. Overburdened with the complexities and deficits inherent in disadvantaged urban life, fueled by repeated failure and lost opportunities, they are filled with self-doubt. Their reticence and reluctance to act reinforces their feeling that life events are beyond their control. In keeping with the natural inclination to preserve the ego, these parents adopt a passive response style, in effect withdrawing from involvement in seemingly threatening situations. School personnel interpret their distance as parental disinterest. Nevertheless, some parents do venture into the social system of the school, accompanied by uncertainties and misgivings.

Initially, when Beatrice Malcolm realized her reading skills were not sufficient for her to continue working informally with a third-grade reading group, she feared telling the teacher and without notice failed to appear for a number of her scheduled group sessions. Repeatedly when contacted, she assured the teacher that she would be there the next day. After a week passed, the teacher took the initiative in suggesting that it would be better to change Ms. Malcolm's assignment to one that would better fit the other demands on her time. Following this, Ms. Malcolm again began keeping her commitment at school but performing other tasks. Many months later, she revealed that she was taking a course in reading in the adult education program.

Ms. Malcolm had been engaged in an assignment that exceeded her capabilities. When parents assist in schools, it is critical that the task they undertake match their abilities and that opportunities to develop competencies are available. This mother's self-esteem was being undermined by threatening circumstances. But given the mutual respect and power of the relationship that had developed over time between Ms. Malcolm and the teacher, Ms. Malcolm could return to the classroom on the strength of belief in her capabilities and in other skills that proved her worth. Out of this experience, her own life was enhanced.

This mother's situation is representative of many other parents whose own development moves to the forefront of their personal agenda by virtue of experience in their children's education. Johnson (1990) cites the grandfather who acknowledges his involvement with his granddaughter's education as a catalyst in his decision to update his own education and to qualify for his general education diploma (GED).

Individuals derive self-esteem from being able to make things happen in their world. A sense of well-being evolves when they overcome obstacles and subsequently savor the satisfaction of goal attainment. Recognition of one's accomplishments by those in power reinforces the individual's determination to develop and pursue personal goals that ultimately can lead to social competency. Each competent act breeds self-confidence and encouragement to go beyond that act, and as success occurs, no matter how little, the cycle continues. With these successes brought about by collaboration, a sense of trust begins to emerge between school personnel and the parent community.

Devising the Parent-School Activity Index

Some activities examined in the model reported in this book are in the tradition of the PTA movement; other modes of participation grew out of the parent-school interaction of the late 1960s and 1970s. The PTA focuses on issues that affect children, schools, and families. In its concern with the well-being of children and youth, one of its primary missions is to assist parents and teachers, both individually and as partners in understanding and meeting children's needs. Recently the PTA has targeted improving home-school cooperation in disadvantaged communities (*PTA Today*, 1991). Both models, however, share the common mission of connecting parents and school. In disadvantaged settings, the process unfolds in different social and economic circumstances.

For parents in poor communities, who represent potential waiting to be developed, many varying processes and modalities are needed to elicit their participation. Structural mechanisms are required to give direction and form to the processes and activities that are basic to participation. These activities represent the core of the parent-school activity index.

In 1974, as part of the initial study, the parent-school activity index was devised based on the judgments of a school-based panel. Seven members of the Baldwin-King School Program, located in a predominately black inner-city neighborhood, were selected as raters. In keeping with the commitment and integrity of the program, it was critical that the scale include the perspective of persons indigenous to the school and/or community. The raters were a principal, two classroom teachers, a parent employed as a school community aide, a school social worker, and two parents, one of whom was a volunteer. They were asked to evaluate and assign a numerical value to eleven designated and defined activities in which parents were actually participating.

The activities and functions rated were gleaned from a survey in which parents and school personnel were asked to indicate all activities and contacts that parents had had with the school since the onset of the six-year-old program. From the list, the eleven categories were generated. Three dimensions were isolated as criteria for evaluating and assigning weights to these activities: time commitment, personal responsibility, and impact of the activity on the day-to-day functioning of the school. Raters worked independently and were instructed to assign a value to each defined activity on the basis of one-time participation. Activities believed to have the strongest combination of the three dimensions would be assigned a value of 5 ranging down to those with the least, which would receive a value of 1. The rating indicated for each category reflects an average of the pooled ratings of the seven raters. The individual ratings were in strong agreement, with an inter-rater reliability coefficient of +.88 (table 4.1).

The Raters

The principal, Mr. Salerno, was a well-seasoned administrator who was particularly sensitive to the needs of the community. He was well regarded by the public school central office administration and highly respected by his constituents in the local community. By the time this initiative was undertaken, he had demonstrated commitment to the concept of school-parent collaboration and had provided six years of leadership for a program dedicated to parent involvement.

One classroom teacher, Mrs. Frederick, a twenty-year veteran of the public school system, was one of the first African American teachers employed by this school system. Initially, she, like the principal, had defined the parents' role in children's education as assistance with homework, fund raising, attending parent-teacher conferences, and special school events; parent involvement as conceived in this model was foreign to her. Yet over time, Mrs. Frederick emerged as an ardent supporter of parents' extended role, and parent volunteers, regularly assisted in her third-grade classroom.

The other classroom teacher had completed two years of elementary school teaching before electing to teach in an inner-city school. Of working-class Scottish background, Ms. McPherson, who at the time of this study had accumulated eight years of teaching, was considered one of the most innovative teachers in the school. She eagerly endorsed program goals.

The position of school-community aide was pivotal. As a paid school employee, Mrs. Higgins enjoyed the status of her position, performing a vital function as advocate and spokesperson for deprived and dysfunctional families. In the initial stages of the program, she had joined other paraprofessionals in the system in circulating a petition protesting the program out of

Table 4–1
ANOVA of Inter-rater Reliability for School Activities, 1975

Source	Sum of Squares	Mean Square (MS)	df
Between items	63.06	6.31	10
Within items	52.03	.79	11(6) = 66
Total	115.09		76

Note: The coefficient of inter-rater reliability (r) over all items and for all raters is given as:

$$r = 1 - \frac{\text{MS within items}}{\text{MS between items}} = 1 - .79 = 1 - .12 = .88.$$

fear that their jobs would be threatened by the advent of parent volunteers. As the years passed with no decrease in the number of paraprofessionals, Mrs. Higgins became a supporter not only of the program but of parents' volunteering in the school.

Mrs. Higgins was especially influential with one of the parent raters, Ms. Canty, a passive and withdrawn woman who, after two years of persistent coaxing and encouragement, had agreed to become a parent volunteer. A single mother, she had three children seven years and under: a boy in the second grade, a girl in kindergarten, and a toddler. She had completed two years as a volunteer in her daughter's classroom. Ms. Canty's duties included assisting the teacher in a variety of activities: passing out and collecting supplies, helping children with and learning to keep track of their belongings, and consoling, comforting, and redirecting children whose unreadiness and fears circumvented learning. In her quiet and reticent manner, she emerged as a strong, settling figure in the classroom, well suited to the demands of these children. With her assistance, the teacher reported being able to expand the expectations for her five- and six-year-old charges.

The other parent, chosen to serve as a rater did not volunteer in the school, although occasionally Ms. Johnson attended special assemblies. She, like Ms. Canty, had three children in the school: one in kindergarten and twins in the fourth grade. Her children were experiencing difficulty, and often the school-community aide had to make several visits before Ms. Johnson would keep an appointment to discuss concerns regarding her children.

Rounding out the panel of raters was the school social worker Ms. Schuman, a young white professional whose appointment to the program was initially challenged by the parents. They questioned her ability to understand and respond to the problems and issues besetting the black community. Five years later, she had become a confidante to a number of parents, a mentor, and a trusted colleague. Many initiatives were implemented under her direction. By the time the parent-school activity index was being processed, she had been instrumental in mounting a number of workshops to prepare school personnel for working with parents in on-site school activities. Participants from school systems across the state attended these workshops.

Activities and Functions

An average of the ratings were assigned to the following activities: classroom assistants and aides, executive committee and advisory board membership, room mother, tutor, workshop participant, field trip monitor, lunchroom assistant, attendance at parent-teacher meetings, fund raising, and participation in social events.

The activities and functions that engage parents directly in the learning process and put them in close proximity to students and teachers during the regular school day received the maximum rating of 5. In this area there is an expected level of independent thought and functioning within the orbit of collaboration. Certain skills are required to carry out these activities, such as literacy, problem solving, goal setting, and decision making. Of the eleven categories, two were assigned the top rating of 5: classroom assistants and executive committee in which parents participate with school personnel in planning and problem solving.

Classroom assistants and aides. In the late 1960s and early 1970s, as an outcome of Title I of the Elementary and Secondary Education Act, some funding was available to schools located in low-income areas to hire and train teacher aides. Head Start was one of the pioneers in acknowledging and utilizing the potential of the mothers of their early childhood charges. Aides hired were usually people indigenous to the community, and in most cases parents of school-age children. Many classroom aides took courses and achieved career advancement as a result of their involvement. Some school systems underwrote the educational costs for these aides or provided release time if they were enrolled in an approved course of study.

The project schools in this study had two paid aides and a number of volunteer aides when the initial program, with its strong parent involvement component, got underway. Ongoing training was an important aspect of this initiative—not only for aides but for teachers, who would no longer be the sole adult in the classroom and, hence, in the eyes of the children, the sole authority. As appropriate roles and functions of aides in instructional settings were emerging, parent volunteers were already performing similar tasks in the classrooms. Issues of territory, related primarily to job security, did arise, but they were quickly attended to. The need for classroom aides or assistants greatly exceeded the capacity of the local school district to provide them, even in the wake of federal funding. Initially, paid and volunteer parents were distinguished as aides and volunteers, respectively; however, as the program developed, divisions blurred, and distinction vanished.

School systems use different nomenclature for parents assisting teachers and students in the classroom. When the study was replicated in Milwaukee in 1987 at the Dawson School, classroom parent volunteers were referred to as *room parents*. In this capacity, a parent assisting in the classroom performs a range of tasks, depending on her skill and ability and the wishes and direction of the teacher. Such tasks included distributing supplies, collecting and correcting papers, monitoring independent desk work, and directly assisting with a science project by enabling a child to carry out an experiment. Parents work with individual children, drilling in phonetics or consoling a distraught kindergartner. A first-grade teacher at the Dawson School set up a corner where parents could read to children at different times throughout the day. The range of tasks depends on the flexibility and ingenuity of the teacher and the abilities and interests of the parents.

Executive committee and advisory board. In this category, encompassing governance, a parent shares in the school's overall planning, goal setting, and decision making. Considered a higher-order activity, it is the only other category given a designation of 5.

In the late 1960s and early 1970s, demands by community groups for participation in policy and decision making in the school system engendered vehement, and sometimes even violent, dissension between communities and schools. Involvement in policy determinations remains a popular and coveted level of participation among the disadvantaged whose experience has been one of exclusion from participation in the development of decisions that affect their lives.

Sharing in the day-to-day management of the school is a critical component of the School Development Program. A management group comprising teachers and parents and led by the principal meets regularly to plan and oversee the school program. It also reviews purchasing decisions. Ideally, the teachers and parents serving on this committee are elected by their peers.

Engaging parents in educational determinations remains a mandate of Head Start, the Comer School Development, and Schools Reaching Out programs. The collective activity conveys the belief that parents warrant a voice in what happens to their children. This recognition by those in positions associated with the power structure promotes a positive self-image in those who view themselves as having less power. When parents have an opportunity to participate in executive and administrative functions and are able to negotiate their way through resistance and turf issues, they emerge with new found self-respect and a sense of accomplishment.

Room mother, tutor, and workshop participant. This area, which supports educational objectives and engages parents directly in helping children or as targeted learners themselves, was given a weight of 4.

The room mother role, in the tradition of the PTA model, differs from that of classroom aide or assistant. The room mother's assignment is peripheral to didactic instruction or takes place outside the classroom. For example, she maintains ongoing contact with the teacher to carry out minor tasks that might involve contacting other parents about special school events or to solicit contributions for school causes. Occasionally, the room mother may help in the classroom in connection with a special event but not on a sustained basis, as is the case with classroom assistants.

A tutor-volunteer with the requisite skills works with an individual child or group of children in developing reading, computational, or other skills. A sustained activity such as tutoring can occur in the classroom, after school, or in school-sponsored tutoring centers located in community facilities.

The presence of those from the community participating in the learning process sends a powerful message of self-efficacy and accountability, not only to themselves but, as important, to their children. Both the professional and local communities see that indigenous citizens have the ability to carry out these tasks.

The activities of these volunteers are monitored through regular contact with teachers. Interaction with classroom teachers on an individual or group basis provides an opportunity for learning and self-development.

Workshops are a vehicle for more formal opportunities for learning and personal development, and they are critical, given the disproportionate number of parents with marginal skills who live in the inner city. The Schools Reaching Out project in Boston included parents in training workshops planned for teachers. In the workshops, both teachers and parents became more sensitive to issues associated with parent-teacher interaction through role playing (Johnson 1990). Workshops can range from an event lasting several successive days, often scheduled during the summer, to biweekly or bimonthly meetings throughout the school year.

Classroom observation, field trips, lunchroom assistance, and parent-teacher meetings. All four of these activities were placed at midrange, with a designation of 3 on the parent-school activity continuum.

Classroom observation, in which parents are invited to witness a lesson or activity, is primarily a spectator activity, and parents are expected to be unobtrusive. The objective can be primarily informational as in back-to-school programs, where parents are exposed to what takes place on an ordinary school day, or parents may be called in to observe in a classroom when their child is experiencing a problem that they have difficulty accepting.

Such was the case with Samara Price, who did not seem to understand the extent of her son's hearing limitations and was resisting referral for an audiological evaluation. When informed by the teacher, she shrugged it off as a minor condition that would pass, noting that Bobby did not have any trouble listening to the "often too loud" television at home. She became convinced when she saw for herself the difficulties he was having in the classroom.

Classroom observation has been used as a component of training to prepare parents for positions as assistants. Teachers are much more comfortable today in having parents observe the instructional enterprise, yet there is the reality of territory and ultimate responsibility and a certain decorum required of observers. Schools have established guidelines governing classroom visitation.

Parents accompanying teachers and students on field trips is another traditional activity. The attention of additional adults on such excursions sends a positive message; it reduces students' inclination to "act out" and reduces the likelihood of accidents and disruptive behavior. Assisting on field trips is usually a one-time endeavor, although the same corps of parents many volunteer on a number of occasions.

In inner-city schools with a disproportionate number of students in subsidized meal programs, most students take their midday meal at school. Lunchtime can reap pandemonium, and cafeteria decorum can leave a lot to be desired. The presence of parent lunchroom monitors has aided in restoring order by sending a clear message of expected behavior. Keeping order is the primary task. Usually there is little interaction between parent monitors and individual children except in the process of restoring order. One exception is a woman who serves as lunchroom monitor in the Dawson School in Milwaukee and uses each lunch period to share with pupils a humorous anecdote about her experience as the only girl on a farm with nine brothers. Even usually restless children listen attentively to her suspenseful humor. She exerts a positive influence on their lives. A similar outcome occurs when parents serve as hall or playground monitors and interact on a regular basis with children.

Another opportunity to utilize parent assistance is on school grounds when children gather, awaiting the start of the school day. Almost daily at the Locust Avenue School, minor skirmishes and fights would break out between children waiting for the school doors to open. As a result, the school day would get off to a hectic start, ushered in by the din of angry, upset, or overly stimulated children and the school personnel trying to calm them. The principal's office was besieged, and a disruptive atmosphere permeated the main corridors, negatively affecting everyone in the school.

Mrs. Odessa Williams, who walked her seven-year-old granddaughter to school, had been observing the mayhem for several months and suggested that she would be willing to serve as a monitor. Parents were notified that there would be a monitor; they were given information about the behavior expected of their children and the consequences if their children did not comply. In below-zero weather that winter, Mrs. Williams, confident in the power of her role as a school-appointed monitor, could be observed at her post maintaining order. The school day was off to a less volatile start with a climate more conducive to learning.

Another area of participation included in this category is attendance at parent-teacher meetings. Parental presence at school-based meetings and social functions is a traditional form of participation. By attending activities and programs that involve exchanges with teachers and principal, parents convey their interest and provide and receive information. This category covers individual conference with teachers or the principal, school meetings, and assembly programs. In the past, parental interaction with schools was focused primarily in this last category of activities.

Fund raising and social events. These two activities were assigned a rating of 2. Both occur on or off the school premises; neither is related closely to the primary instructional task of schools.

Bake sales and raffles, traditionally popular ways to raise money in schools, can provide some financial support for a classroom or all-school special activity. Walk marathons and commercially sponsored cookie and candy sales are other activities parents endorse to raise money. These activities are sporadic and usually occur once in a school year. Other social events, such as school potluck suppers and special holiday celebrations, project a feeling of camaraderie and may involve intense and sustained effort, but they have minimal impact on instruction or the day-to-day interactions that occur in the school.

Additional activities can be developed by creative and committed parents and teachers. For example, parents in Milwaukee, under the guidance of the school social worker, instituted a telephone support network for children who were at home alone several hours before a parent arrived from work.

A composite of the ratings for each set of activities on the parent-school activity index yields a score that is used to explore parent involvement in relation to sociodemographic factors and dimensions of alienation. It was my belief that parents whose participation was high were less likely to agree with the statements characterizing alienation than parents whose participation was low. In devising the index, the total score of 38 was divided into three categories: low activity scores 0–7; moderate activity scores 8–13; and high activity scores, 14–38. The high participation scores were set low to reflect reality, since the upper ranges represent a rarely achieved ideal. Even with this accommodation, significant differences in responses were found between those with low participant scores and those with high participant scores.

It is difficult to codify parent-school activities, given the variation in the types and levels of responsibilities that parents may assume. This is so whether the involvement of parents directly encompasses the didactic process of learning, provides support in assisting children to control disruptive behavior, or functions to assist teachers with the nuts and bolts associated with instruction. At best, the index serves as a general broad indicator and does not distinguish regular and consistent activity from one-time or sporadic parent participation.

Even though parents in the control school had served on advisory committees or similar boards as part of Head Start or federally funded programs, their participation in executive-type activities was significantly less than that of parents in the Baldwin-King School Program, with its commitment to implementing comprehensive program of shared decision making and participatory planning (table 4.2).

Activities that differed significantly in participation between the two schools were an executive committee, participation in workshops, and tutoring. In activities such as accompanying children and school personnel on field trips and attending parent-teacher meetings, long the more traditional avenues of participation, there also were significant differences between the schools.

The index also was used in 1987 to explore the participation of mothers of children attending three inner-city elementary schools in Milwaukee that

Table 4–2
Distribution of Parent Participation in School Activities, 1975

Weight	Activity/Function	*Percentage of Parents Participating*		*t* value	*df*	*p*
		Jones Street School (N = 80)	*Baldwin-King School* (N = 80)			
5	Executive or school advisory committee	12.5	25	2.03	158	.05
	Classroom assistant or aide	5.0	10	1.20	158	n.s.
4	Workshop participant	46.2	63.7	2.24	158	.05
	Tutor	3.7	13.7	2.26	158	.05
	Room mother	11.2	17.5	1.12	158	n.s.
3	Field trips	23.7	38.7	2.06	158	.05
	Parent-teacher meetings	78.7	88.7	1.72	158	.05
	Lunchroom assistance	8.7	6.3	−.60	158	n.s.
	Classroom observation	55.0	47.5	−.95	158	n.s.
2	Social events	18.8	66.2	6.89	158	.001
	Fund-raising	46.2	78.7	4.48	158	.001

had undertaken a concentrated pilot program of parent involvement. In the later study, both populations of mothers who were compared—high- and low-frequency participants—were in the same school. High-frequency participant mothers were more likely than low-frequency mothers to reject the alienation statements. Factors such as educational level, marital status, and number of children, also influenced their responses.

5
Parents on the Research Team

The process and exchange that takes place when parents have a responsible role in research serves to minimize distrust and reduce alienation. The concept of involving parents in school-based research was and still is relatively novel. The challenge was to carry out a process that maintained methodological integrity while respecting and negotiating the contributions of the parent team members. A number of social, political, and economic factors influenced the process.

African Americans and Research

The history of research in this country does not hold fond memories for African Americans as subjects, although researchers over the years have demonstrated increasing sensitivity to their subjects' reactions and concerns. Nevertheless, skepticism still prevails toward survey research, census data collection, and social, behavioral, political, or medical research endeavors.

The discontent with research, which peaked in the late 1960s and early to mid-1970s, ranged from a mass protest that resulted in the Bureau of the Census's discarding a question about the presence of flush toilets in homes to the politicalization that permanently altered a major research university's relationship with its host inner city. The intent of the census question was to determine the extent and depth of poverty and deprivation in the nation. In the university situation, the outcry by citizens was in response to the implementation of a study of adolescent health among poor blacks in New York City's Harlem. Armed with funds from the Children's Bureau in 1967, the Columbia University School of Public Health undertook a study designed as a follow-up of adolescent health patterns. Proceeding in the wake of a comprehensive family health survey that had enjoyed a cooperative response in the same community, unexpectedly the Columbia team was vociferously challenged, with activists calling on the community to withdraw from the study

70

noting that, as subjects, they were not receiving benefits in proportion to their participation (Josephson 1970).

Given the social and political climate at the time, the targeted poor black community was not immune to the indignation driving civil eruptions in a number of major cities in the country. Although many of the sit-ins and demonstrations were not reactions to research activities per se, they embodied the general outrage and frustrations endured by black and other poor people. Academic researchers conducting studies in poor communities were more available targets than the amorphous and distant policymakers. Poor African Americans, already destitute and disadvantaged, earmarked for what they perceived as esoteric research that promised little benefit for them, confronted and challenged the principal investigators (Costello 1973).

In the Columbia study, the investigators surmised that the opposition leaders were a militant activist community group with their own agenda. Nonetheless, local opposition to the study mounted when several black professionals affiliated with the Columbia study deserted the ranks of the university-based research group and took up the mantle of protest. These circumstances occurred in the context of the community's perception of Columbia University's monolithic posture in the community (the town-gown issue) and the civil rights movement nationwide.

The Columbia investigators inferred that "most people in Harlem ... knew little about the survey or if they did, were indifferent" to it (Josephson 1970:124). The comment, a callous prejudgment of the local populations' lack of knowledge or unfamiliarity with the study, is precisely the issue. The indifference cited can be viewed as a maneuver to mask insecurities and vulnerabilities.

Potential subjects of empirical investigation who are unfamiliar with the purpose of research and its procedures are frequently less educated and need to be informed and engaged, if only to gain their cooperation. The fact that there is a commitment to the higher order of an added educational value must be made clear to the subjects. Powerful outcomes can be anticipated from such exchange. The resistance of the central Harlem community resonated with the pervasive feelings of alienation and powerlessness frequently expressed by many African Americans, overtly and covertly. Defiance surfaces as a visible ramification of alienation and a healthy response to indifference.

The reaction by both the professional and indigenous community to the 1965 report on the Negro family by Daniel Moynihan was a forerunner of the mounting discontent during that period. Both liberals and black scholars decried the findings in the report that highlighted pathological functioning among a large number of African American families in urban ghettos. The publicity extended to the report fueled the resentment of an already beleaguered African American population. The atmosphere did not encourage empathic social scientists to undertake research based on poor black life. Instead, "the controversy surrounding the Moynihan report had the effect of curtailing serious research on minority problems in the inner-city for over a decade" (Wilson 1987:4). Wilson reminds us that while black and sympathetic scholars shied away from such research, conservative thinkers forged ahead, and a body of one-sided research studies resulted that did not advance the cause of underprivileged African Americans. This unfavorable atmosphere for social research lasted throughout the 1970s.

Coinciding with the outrage and demonstrations of discontent during the early 1970s was the publicizing of the Tuskegee Syphilis Study that had been going on since 1932 under the auspices of the U.S. Public Health Service. The Tuskegee experiment had been undertaken "to determine the natural course of untreated, latent syphilis in black males." Seventy-four of the original four hundred syphilitic black men in the study were still living in 1972, and even with the easy access to penicillin by the early 1950s, they were medically monitored but not treated for their condition. Such racially driven policies and practices punctuated the alienation and self-estrangement of these victims of imposed social isolation and the alienation of other African Americans who viewed themselves similarly vulnerable to such unethical practices. It is estimated that more than one hundred black men who were included in the study died directly from advanced, untreated syphilitic lesions (Brandt 1978). In 1972, forty years after the start of the experiment, the study was halted by the Department of Health, Education and Welfare in the wake of national publicity. It was only then that this ethical travesty became public, and a panel to investigate was appointed.

The syphilis study remains one of the more blatant examples of national disregard and nationally sanctioned exploitation executed in the name of scientific inquiry. Knowledge about this racially based study, wrought with deception and disregard for human life, became grist for the antiestablishment polarization of the 1970s. This experience heightened the suspicion and mistrust that African Americans harbored about research, and such attitudes transferred to other areas. Distrust generated by insensitively conceived and executed research was not limited to African Americans but was shared by other minorities.

Head Start: Confounding Statistical Reports

At the same time, the highly visible and successful Project Head Start, with its strong presence in poor urban and rural communities, suffered the contradictions of varying statistical findings. This comprehensive early childhood program for economically disadvantaged preschool children and their families had been the subject of publicly mandated and privately supported evaluation and research studies. Focusing in 1969 on whether a child's cognitive development was positively affected by the Head Start experience, the Westinghouse Learning Cooperation reported that after a few years in elementary school, children lost the gains made in Head Start.

A number of more comprehensive studies subsequently targeted a range of outcomes related to Head Start program goals and objectives. One of them, the Lasting Effects Study, revealed a consistency of results, thus affirming the positive outcomes (Glazer 1988).

Head Start was affiliated closely with community-based antipoverty programs. Given the programs' large number of African American and minority children, it is not hard to imagine that the debate about the research findings challenging the benefits of Head Start was a threat to parents, many of whom worked in or were otherwise closely associated with the program. Along with local administrators and teachers, the hopes and dreams of many parents have been placed in Head Start's potential. Some viewed the statistical manipulations as a deliberate attempt to discredit an effective program.

The Standardized Test Debate

Educational research that compares performance on standardized tests across racial groups has long been a sensitive area for blacks. The much-disputed Jensen biogenetic theory promulgated in the 1960s in an attempt to explain the differences between white and black academic performance in terms of innate racial differences incurred widespread scholarly debate and popular visibility. Jensen's theory threatened to discredit the cultural deprivation theory and the education policy and compensatory programs grounded in that theory. Challenging Jensen on the basis of flaws in his theoretical formulations and methodology, Ogbu (1978) demonstrated that the Jensen theory does not adequately explain differences in black-white academic performance. Ogbu further suggested that "the policy implication of Jensen's theory is likely to reinforce the very factors that cause black-white differences" (p. 64). The ensuing scholarly discourse and debate in the popular press, community meetings, and even religious forums raised the ire and increased suspicion among the African American community.

Changing Attitudes

Blacks have been the most systematically studied racial ethnic minority group in the United States. For decades, they have been the subject of social, political, and medical research. But the hope and implied promise that outcomes would yield improvement in their condition have been unfulfilled. Challenging the lopsided payoff, indigenous citizens voiced their discontent with such research. They perceived the dominant society as inflicting upon the minority society a process that had little relevance to their suffering and deficit-laden existence.

Yet from these experiences, the poor became persistent in their determination to influence their destiny through participation and/or input into planning and execution of human service and educational programming.

Through ongoing, although often embattled, exchange between policymakers and local citizens, perceptions were clarified and goals modified. As community residents became closer to those who recommended, made, or implemented policy, both parties questioned, communicated, and learned more, and research, policies, and programs met with greater success.

Response of the Research Community

Researchers during the 1970s were not deaf to the sentiments held by poor and minority groups. Some investigators began to assess research initiatives in poor, minority communities with a different type of lens. A thrust borne of pragmatism for some and genuine concern for others became more evident. Theoretical formulations, methodological processes, and interpretation of findings were evaluated in a different context (Bengtson et al. 1977). A body of scholarly studies surfaced that probed the sensitive issues surrounding research being carried out in disadvantaged urban communities (Zinn 1979).

The principal investigators of the Columbia University and Children's Bureau–sponsored study, who initially misjudged the passions of a so-called indifferent community, later identified a number of broader research questions for analysis. Of major concern was the heretofore unanticipated implications of studying deviant or pathological behavior in a disadvantaged community. Although uncertain as to what point in the process indigenous input should occur, they identified the need for community participation in social science research.

An array of social science literature that critically examined the research process, presentation of outcomes, and the interaction between principal investigators and subjects surfaced in the 1970s (Zinn 1979). Theoretical formulations and fundamental assumptions that formerly yielded distorted interpretations and misrepresentations were called into question. Central to the discourse was the significance of race in the research enterprise. In survey research, for example, questions addressing issues such as the extent to which the race of the interviewer influenced outcomes demanded consideration. Factors such as language and cultural specificity permeate all facets of the research enterprise as potently as do hypothesis formulation, methodology, empirical issues, and dissemination of findings.

In the disquieting atmosphere of this period, some black scholars maintained that only black scholars should conduct research in black communities. Their basic premise was that as blacks, they shared an affinity with and thus understood the community and culture. This belief fueled the insider-outsider debate that flourished in sociological circles in the 1970s. Merton (1972) characterized insiders as those claiming to have a monopoly on knowledge and special insights concerning a particular group. The outsiders, however, asserted that only those external to a group can have objective, unbiased knowledge about the group. While Merton appealed for the factions to unite, his treatise was viewed by black and racially ethnic scholars as failing to address critical methodological and empirical issues pertinent to the populations in question. Cogent realities such as the negative perception of research held by ethnic and minority groups and their hostility were not included in his analysis (Zinn 1979).

National survey research that used interviewers indigenous to the community tended to reduce problems perpetuated by differences in social class and language usage (Jackson, Tucker, and Bowman 1982). But although shared ethnicity and race between principal investigators and subjects can have a positive effect on the research exchange and can transmit a more inclusive message to research subjects, it is no panacea; minority researchers still encounter problems. Nevertheless, the social scientists actively engaged during this period did ascertain that different questions were posed when local interviewers were used, foreseeing the eventuality of different answers being discovered (Blauner and Wellman 1973). Similarly, in their collaborative study of the aged population, Bengtson and his colleagues (1977) found that the responsiveness and involvement of the community did not lessen the goals of the researcher to acquire new knowledge. Rather, they demonstrated that the input of the diverse community—Anglo, African American and Mexican American, and the elderly—strengthened the validity and thus the interpretive capability of the data.

African American scholars were joined by their Hispanic, Asian, and white counterparts concerned about issues related to the efficacy of research in disadvantaged communities. Of particular consequence was methodology. In research circles, certain activities are more valued and are thus more jealously guarded than others. Hypothesis formulation and construction of research questions are examples. When action or field research is to be undertaken, empirical generalizations are made and questions to be asked are framed a priori, by principal investigators. An outcome during this decade of transition was the inclusion of indigenous or special populations in some aspect of the initial processes. As constituents became more politically astute and informed, it was pragmatic to garner and incorporate their input at the onset. Making the transition from traditional research procedures to methodologies that acknowledge, value, and incorporate indigenous input, albeit time-consuming and wrought with tension, is a worthwhile challenge.

Traditional research paradigms cannot be "simply translated" into a viable community model (Bengtson et al. 1977:88). Action-oriented research presupposes a problem-solving initiative. The intent of applied research is to solve some practical problems by influencing economic, political, or social policy formulation. Considerable allocation of institutional resources, both monetary and in-kind, professional and personal commitment, accompanies such undertakings. The outcomes have the potential of redirecting the lives and altering the future of those who are disadvantaged. It is important that the same weight and importance be given to the dynamics of meetings and relationship processes where interpretations and training occur as to research design and hypothesis formulation.

It is no longer uncommon for populations earmarked for social research to be involved in initial planning and decision making. As we enter their social milieu, it is with informed caution, willingness to listen, and a commitment to engage. Early interaction and exchange between principal investigators and the subject population builds a foundation of trust and mutual respect and permits flexibility in planning and construct development, therefore resulting in an avoidance of conflict associated with earlier programs.

Analysis of a Participatory Model*

Disorder, suspicion, and disillusionment characterized the national and local climate in 1973 when the initial model engaging parents as research team members was undertaken. The primary objective of the endeavor was to develop an evaluation, which would include the parents' perspective, of a public school intervention program that had been ongoing since 1968. Paralleling a primary objective and commitment of the program planners, parents would be an integral part of the evaluation process.

The program had been founded on the premise that forces occurring within the social system of the school that interfered with learning could be altered. By synthesizing mental health and child development concepts with educational processes, growth-producing educational environments would evolve. Traditional hierarchical arrangements separating school administrators, teachers, and parents could be modified. Parents would become an integral part of the day-to-day activities of the school, including a meaningful role in planning. A consensual decision-making process would mediate differences. A more participatory social system was the anticipated outcome.

With this commitment, the Yale University Child Study Center and the New Haven public school system entered a partnership requesting funding from the Ford Foundation to support an intervention program to be implemented in two inner-city schools. Both the Child Study Center and the school system, who shared responsibility for operating the Baldwin-King School Program, received its own funding. At its inception, the program was directed jointly by Dr. James Comer and a senior administrator from the school system's superintendent's office.

Inclusion of parents at all levels of decision making had been a primary goal of the Baldwin-King School Program. Located in the university's med-

---

*Based on the author's doctoral dissertation, "Black Mothers in Urban Schools," submitted to Yale University in 1975.

ical complex, the Child Study Center's program initiatives encompass service, training, and research. Its nursery school enjoys a national and international reputation. The university, situated in the midst of the central city, intersects with a number of poor predominantly African American neighborhoods.

At its inception, the program began in two schools with a black student population exceeding 90 percent—one a kindergarten through fourth grade and the other kindergarten through sixth grade. It was anticipated that additional schools in the local school system would be included over the years. The designers of the program intended that the union between the university and the public school system would approximate parity. However, equitable funding did not mitigate the university's historically powerful position in the community. Similar to the experience of other research institutions attempting to implement community-based programs during this period, there was fundamental skepticism regarding the university's motivations.

The first years of the program were chaotic and a challenge to all participants. Teacher and parent distrust of the Yale Child Study Center team was evident, as was their distrust of one another. In the early stage of contemplating a parent assessment of the program, some school personnel felt threatened and became defensive about a parent survey. They were uncomfortable with a process they viewed as an evaluation of their performance. The wisdom of having parents evaluate teachers even indirectly was questioned. Some teachers believed that a negative response was to be expected.

Although emphasis was on the parent involvement objective of the program, inquiries as to whether a parent had ever been encouraged by school personnel to participate in school activities did focus on the relationships with teachers and other school staff. Similarly, a question exploring the extent to which a parent felt free to discuss concerns with school personnel highlighted interaction involving teachers. A question to ascertain the frequency with which parents conferred with teachers directly targeted them. Other questions inquired about the school's role in motivating children to succeed academically and to aspire for high goals. Inquiries regarding the acquisition of basic skills sought to evaluate educational outcomes from the parents' perspective. Teachers were assured that the parents would be selected at random, that no particular classroom was targeted, and that neither teachers nor parent respondents would be identified.

The Child Study Center team suffered moments of distrust and breakdown in communication too. James Comer, the director who kept the team on track toward the goal, poignantly details the early days of the program in *School Power* (1980). But after several years, the discontinuities experienced at the onset of the program were replaced by the interplay of acknowledging and resolving differences in order to realize mutually agreed upon goals.

The commitment to involve parents resonated with my earlier experience in working with parents as a school social worker in Head Start. As chief social worker of the Baldwin-King School Program, I worked with these parents daily. Interaction included informal exchanges in the corridors and more formal exchanges during teacher conferences, classroom meetings, or when parents assisted teachers in classrooms, tutored children, or performed other services in the school. Ideas and information were exchanged when parents took part in program-sponsored workshops on educational issues, tutoring, and child care or on handling troublesome behavior. Parents who were overwhelmed by or unable to deal adequately with home situations or their own children's problems were helped on an individual basis in the school or referred to community agencies or more extensive services provided by the Yale Child Study Center. Given the program's mission to disseminate information to other school systems, parents assisted with and participated in special workshops sponsored for professional groups, school personnel, and parents from across the state. The program orchestrated ongoing interaction between teachers, parents, and Child Study Center professionals in a range of activities and in a number of capacities.

The parents' activity in the day-to-day process of the school, their interaction and exchange with classroom teachers, and their dialogue with Child Study Center staff furthered their knowledge and information about schools, educational processes, and what makes for supportive environments. The exchange was reciprocal; teachers and Child Study Center staff learned and gained valuable insights from parents who questioned and challenged. Maintaining clear and open channels of communication proved to be an ongoing and worthwhile challenge.

One area that benefited was that concerning standardized tests. Traditionally the children in the program schools had tested in the lowest percentile. Evaluation had been an ongoing part of the program. Workshops and efforts to keep parents informed served to stimulate their curiosity. Parents became more knowledgeable concerning the testing of their children, both in terms of school-generated and standardized tests. By 1980 the performance of fourth graders had reached the fiftieth percentile (Comer 1988). Although still ambivalent about the efficacy of standardized tests and other evaluative measures that they saw as pigeonholing their children and perhaps even an evaluation of themselves, parents were becoming more pragmatic. They began to recognize testing, whether standard or teacher generated, as being intrinsic to the educational process and necessary if their children were going to be prepared to compete.

In preparation for the "parents-as-consumers" evaluation, one facet of a number of assessments, the entire school community had been briefed in several meetings of the plan for and objectives of the survey. Procedures, methodology, and planned utilization of the findings were explained to parents in detail.

Selecting Informants

After conferring with the principals, teachers, teacher aides, Child Study Center staff, and parent volunteers, it was agreed that parent informants would be those who were involved in some level of school activities. Involvement could be cursory and limited to attendance at open school sessions, teacher conferences, major school functions such as parent-teacher meetings, and special performances by the children. At the other end of the participatory continuum, informants could be parents who attended workshops and training sessions and regularly volunteered in the classroom or assisted with major school events. A parent informant could be a member of the program's governing board or hold an office in the parent-teacher organization. However, an informant could not be an employee of the school or program. The objective was to have informants who reflected a range of parental experience, activity, and commitment.

Little difficulty was encountered in attracting candidates. Once the word was out, many more parents indicated interest and applied than was anticipated. The participatory and inclusive ethos demonstrated over the previous five years had advanced a sense of belonging, which accounted in part for the large number of parents applying to be partners in this endeavor. Ten parent informants were selected. Their educational levels ranged from eighth grade to one parent who had completed some college courses. All were articulate and able to hold their own in what subsequently turned out to be an informative and challenging debate.

Candidates for parent-informant were individually interviewed and given an overview of the objectives of the evaluation and procedures to be used. During these meetings, one parent shared her fear that her neighbors would accuse her of trying to be "big stuff." A Korean War veteran father who later dropped out of the study due to illness found the experience a "new opportunity" in an existence he labeled as "drab." The majority of parents approached the individual session in a guarded fashion, reticent but receptive. Their retiring stance disappeared when the first group meeting was held. The mix and dynamics resulted in a lively exchange, wrought with challenge of the principal investigator, each other, and the program objectives and accomplishments thus far. An agenda including the dates, times, and places of group meetings was established. Two of the informants worked or had other daytime commitments, so the group usually met at night or on occasion on the weekend. A few meetings were held in a community facility near the school. The parents understood that in keeping with program goals, this component of the program evaluation was designed to highlight their perspective.

Constructing the Questionnaire

The commitment to capture what parents deemed important, how they viewed the program's objectives, and what educational outcomes they valued was integral to the program evaluation. The intent was to distinguish what parents valued in the educational process. Questions would reflect their perceptions, albeit subjective, rather than the more objective tradition of relating outcomes to the formal goals of program design. Different questions were being asked in other ongoing evaluations.

It was hypothesized that the parents' perceptions would most likely approximate those of the program designers. Over the years, by virtue of ongoing participation and socialization, parents had been exposed to and had begun to embody the goals and values that characterized the program. This particular evaluation modality focused on what parents deemed as priority.

Although evaluation was undertaken with a nonprofessional group as primary research assistants, an effort was made to adhere to the boundaries of acceptable empirical methodology. During the item construction phase, parents had been directed to think about three general questions that were posed to elicit concerns that would serve as the framework for the interview schedule. One question, "What are the three most important things the program has accomplished to date?" stimulated brainstorming and discussion of what the parents valued as outcomes. The second question, "When you heard about the program, what did you think was going to happen?" served to elicit discussion of their realistic expectations and their fantasies. Hopes and ideals were being sought from a population who suffered the deficits of disadvantage. They were encouraged to acknowledge their dreams. From the articulation of their expectations, their fears were revealed. Some believed that when the program started, "they and their children were guinea pigs in an experiment" and would be abandoned when data were obtained. Few remembered having or acknowledged any positive thoughts at the time. They recalled feeling that they did not have any choice as to whether the program would go forward. Even when the intent of the articulated goal of parent involvement was demonstrated by actions, parents could not envision a reality in which they would have a voice in school operations. Their options and expectations had been minimized by the paucity of their life experiences, thus diminishing their hope. A third question to explore their future goal expectations inquired, "If you could get three things changed in the schools, what would you want?" The content of these discussions became the background for the questionnaire that the parents used when they conducted the interviews.

The exchange in generating the interview schedule was one of the most challenging and gratifying aspects of this project. The feelings in the 1970s were of articulated mistrust and caution, yet these parents wanted to know, and their enthusiasm was contagious. They craved information. By virtue of involvement in this process, they were able to learn how participation and information can affect and generate educational policy. Their questions challenged me to find ways to clarify and articulate concepts that educators and social scientists often take for granted.

The early sessions were burdened by the number of ideas for questions. This was resolved partially when the intricacies of question formulation surfaced and the necessity to adhere to a certain format was discussed. One was how to ensure that people are answering the question posed (item validity) and the importance of getting the same response if the question was repeated (item reliability). They were curious about the connotation of words like *subjects* and *control* that differed from common usage. Often when the content was too technical, they became lost in cumbersome explanations, yet they listened intently to the differences between structured and unstructured interviews and the advantages and disadvantages of both. The long-term relationship and visibility based on my ongoing affiliation with the program facilitated consensus.

After lengthy discussion, a majority of parent-informants insisted that they would not solicit income information from their neighbors. One parent lamented that their children play in the same garbage-laden streets, live in the same project, and were all receiving public assistance. Why ask the obvious? Although all members lived in the same barren, deficit-ridden communities, there was much variance in life-style. Some were caring parents who provided support and an adequate home within their limited means. Others, overburdened by the unrelenting demands of a meager subsistence, struggled to keep their heads above water. And then there were those who succumbed to despair, their lives characterized by alcohol and drug abuse, family violence, and abject familial dysfunctioning. Although arguments were offered to dispute the generalities and to highlight individuality and differences even among those who appear similar and share socioeconomic class, these parents were not convinced. Their discussion of the issue centered around generalizations that stereotype and can prove dysfunctional for a targeted group.

It was clear that the group was uncomfortable and uneasy about obtaining information about income, although they admitted to their common economically disadvantaged status. In the end, specific information regarding income was excluded, but questions about employment status and occupation remained. Census tract data confirmed that a majority of the students came from low-income families that met the federal criteria for funds earmarked for economically deprived children (Winters 1975).

Also included in the questionnaire were three constructs from the sociological literature to ascertain the extent of alienation. Subjects were asked whether they agreed or disagreed with the following statements. "*Meaninglessness:* Things have become so complicated in the world today, I really don't understand what is going on. *Normlessness:* In order to get ahead in the world today, you are almost forced to do some things that are not right. *Powerlessness:* There is not much I can do about most of the important problems that we face today" (Seeman 1959). Parents understood that the statements were standardized and that the language and presentation must remain as it was stated.

After a number of revisions, a fifty-five-item schedule, including questions to elicit demographic data, was the outcome of extensive parental input. This interview schedule was used to assess parent-school activity at the end of six years of the initial program in 1975 and in the 1987 study.

Conducting the Interviews

Parents were particularly responsive to training that emphasized techniques in encouraging interviewees to respond to questions, how to probe for more complete answers, and how to avoid offering one's own opinion. Parent-informants were helped to understand the importance of maintaining neutrality and not succumbing to the urge to coach the respondent. Repeatedly, they were reminded there was no right answer and that we were interested in the range of parental response. But they had been raised in the tradition of right and wrong answers, and the temptation to influence an answer that approximated their own preference persisted. After much practice, cajoling, and reference to the validity of the study being in jeopardy, they reached an acceptable stage of distancing themselves.

Each parent role-played several videotaped interviews and in concert with peers was able to reflect on and evaluate his or her own performance. This exercise enabled the Yale Child Study Center team to ascertain where instruction needed to be personalized.

From the exchange, valuable information was gleaned regarding process and compromise when involving constitutents in research. It is a time-consuming undertaking, demanding flexibility in allowing the process to unfold but not relinquishing responsibility for maintaining methodological integrity. The researcher is exposed to a questioning of that which we take for granted, coupled with the challenge of explaining, in plain language, why we do things the way we do. Learning for all was facilitated. Professionals emerged with more appreciation for the sensitivities, commitment, and natural skills the parent-informants were bringing to the process. Parent-informants surfaced with skills appropriate to and honed for this task.

As the time for the survey approached, fears were reawakened among the parent population. They were uneasy about the intended purpose of the evaluation and use of the findings. Would parents who did not participate be vulnerable in some way? Would personal information be given to local authorities?

A number of parents new to the school community had missed meetings held the previous fall in which the research protocol was presented and explained. Other parents grew more interested as the school year progressed. Therefore, in the spring just prior to the starting date, the pending study and plan for implementation was reviewed in open meetings where questions were raised, concerns and challenges addressed, and program plans for the new school year discussed. With the school community apprised of the survey in a number of written notices and school meetings, interviews were conducted in the parents' homes. As community residents, the parent-interviewers were familiar with and recognized in the neighborhoods.

Just prior to the time when the evaluation was to get underway, I unexpectedly received a National Mental Health Predoctoral Research Award and was able to compensate parent-interviewers. The award, in essence shared with the interviewers in the form of a stipend, enhanced the already positive commitment on their part. They were truly teammates, respected and rewarded.

Feedback from parent-interviewers informed program initiatives. One parent reported being stopped in the hallway of a project by a parent whose name had not been drawn in the sampling. She accused the interviewer of being "in cahoots" with the school, which had "handpicked" the people they wanted to interview. Her own disappointment and rejection was shrouded in her unyielding diatribe. The interviewer denied that the parents had been handpicked. She explained that the process was similar "to putting every parent's name in a hat ... each parent had the same chance of being selected." Another parent suggested she was not chosen because her children got poor report cards. Another blamed the teacher who "just didn't like me since I told her off." The parent-interviewers were able to tell these parents that none of these reasons pertained; "It was the luck of the draw."

What became apparent was the disappointment expressed by a number of parents who were not included. In response, a shorter fifteen-item questionnaire was made available so that parents who were not interviewed could provide feedback. Although the return was modest, parents saw this as a positive move to solicit their opinions. By making programmatic shifts and earmarking areas for development based on the findings, the purpose and value of the consumer evaluation was demonstrated to parents and the school community at large. Information regarding parent perceptions and what they deemed as important added an important dimension to the direction of the program.

By the mid-1980s when the study was replicated in Milwaukee, the social and political climate had changed. This was a more quiescent period with wavering economic security. Two years following the implementation of a pilot parent involvement program in three Milwaukee inner-city elementary schools, a team of parents and school social workers interviewed parents without fanfare. The evaluation was accepted by teachers and parents. Prior approval had been received from the central office administration, a requirement of all research or evaluations carried out in the system.

Current Research and Evaluation Trends

Social and behavioral scientists continue to grapple with the tension inherent in research initiatives carried out among those who are disadvantaged. Much has been learned since the challenges of the 1960s and 1970s. Scholarly literature now addresses a range of issues that focus on reactions of and implications for subjects to research. No longer is the issue whether subjects or clients should have a role in research endeavors; rather, the form that interaction should take is paramount. In spite of fluctuations since its development in the 1940s and 1950s, action research has regained importance. The view of the action research approach as mobilizing people around tasks of problem definition and fact finding has fostered "a form of empowerment and action" that resonates with the participatory ethos of human nature (Sommer 1987:186).

A comprehensive work by Marin and Marin (1991) explores dimensions of research methodology in terms of the implications for Hispanic populations. Much of what is manifest represents similar issues for other minorities. Terminology such as *research participant, client,* and *evaluation* appears side by side with the more classical nomenclature—*respondent, subject,* and *study.* They underscore the value of including community members in all stages of a study: planning, design, analysis, interpretation, and publication. Even the more cerebral research-associated intellectualization and conceptualization that precedes concrete planning and instrument construction is no longer sacrosanct. Where evaluation is integral to any research design, acknowledgment of the consumer's role is requisite. Further along in the process of determining outcome measures, the relationship between perceptual (the client's view) and objective (the researcher's view) requires ongoing analysis and modification (Hougland 1988). These examples are representative of demonstrated commitment to expand the ramifications and acceptance of empirical research.

Research affiliated with initiatives that are favorable at the onset and is undertaken to identify growth and development is readily accepted. In a study by James Rosenbaum of the Northwestern University Center for Urban Affairs and Policy Research that tracked African American student development following families' move to court-ordered subsidized suburban housing, an initial positive response accompanied the families' relocation to more favorable housing. This approving attitude influences support of research that focuses on the outcome of the program (*Chicago Tribune* 1991). In contrast, when constituents feel inadequate and demoralized and fear negative outcomes by virtue of their social position, they are less likely to accept research initiatives. A number of social researchers earnestly seek to facilitate a mutually beneficial process.

Nevertheless, although positive models of research collaboration have been identified, skepticism and mistrust still persists, particularly at the grassroots level. Cruel experiences are not easily eradicated. The reactions of racially ethnic minorities, the disenfranchised, the homeless, the elderly, and other subgroups in resisting the 1990 U.S. census characterize the continuing suspicion and fear regarding surveys among the nation's more vulnerable citizenry. Social and behavioral scientists have progressed in broadening the basis of understanding, acceptance, research inclusivity, and respect for subject sensitivity, but challenges remain that require ongoing diligence. Undoubtedly, research involving disadvantaged populations will take different forms and will forge new alliances as shifts occur in the social, economic, and political structure.

The educational sector with its diverse population and encompassing mandate that includes commitment to evaluation, measurement, and research is the ideal setting for moving in this direction. The very nature of educational institutions belies separation. Schools are not isolated conclaves. Rather, they are dynamic entities affected by interacting social, economic, and political forces.

6
On Mediating Alienation

Urban Life, Disconnectedness, and School Interaction

The urban terrain, defined by disadvantage, isolation, and the scourge of drugs, is the backdrop for the parent participation examined in this book. Crime, chronic under- and unemployment, teenage pregnancies, violent death of the young, deteriorating housing, boarded-up buildings, and homelessness are visible indicators of social disintegration. The personal insult experienced in grappling with the brutal realities of urban life cannot be exaggerated. Overarching this confrontation is the persistent and continuing reality of institutional racism that straddles socioeconomic status. For those without resources and connectedness, racism proves even more harsh. "Enforced alienation" by virtue of skin color, the thesis of Keniston's work in a 1965 monograph, is pertinent here. Alienation in the context of his work is represented as the by-product of racism that breeds psychological damage and a dysfunctional social and environmental milieu. A demoralizing socioenvironmental structure emerges as the primary arena for shaping attitudes and values and fashioning behavior.

Within these communities live the families who are served by inner-city schools. Many appear to be devoid of the personal attachments and interdependent associations common to communities. For many families, their daily needs go unmet. This is particularly so for the families of the nation's 66,000 homeless children who, during some point in 1989, were not able to attend school because they had no permanent residence (Bogart and Le Tendre 1991). Television documents daily the sordid reality of life amid escalating poverty and unrelenting drug-related crime and violence. Yet within these barren conclaves live a number of black families who share the basic American values of work, education, and family. Daily, they strive to carry out these functions against great odds although often outpaced and alienated by the harsh social and economic realities.

Spanning two and a half decades, Alyce Ennis has been a parent participant sufficiently long that the children she guided and assisted are now the parents of students attending the Kilgore-Putnam School in the District of Columbia, where she is the parent coordinator. Her participation predates the inauguration of Head Start in 1965. At the time, she responded to the principal's request for parent volunteers for a preschool program in the school where her two older children were attending. In return, her two preschoolers were registered in the program. Two years later, Mrs. Ennis became a Head Start volunteer. Several years after being in that program, she earned a paid position as a school aide. She and her husband, a mechanic, of forty years live in the same house that they purchased thirty years ago. The neighborhood has changed. No longer is it the close community where parents knew what their children were doing and "kept after them." Windows are barred. Porches, once the center of family and community interaction in warmer seasons, remain empty. Drug-related activity and violence are common. Yet every day, Mrs. Ennis can be found at school, continuously on the move: consoling distraught children, calming angry parents, monitoring the cafeteria, or answering the telephone. Her presence is valued by school personnel, children, and parents alike. She is disheartened and puzzled by the attitudes and values of the teenage mothers who were once her students: "Their behavior isn't right ... they don't believe in anything ... they don't behave in ways that set good examples for their children." Mrs. Ennis speaks of their lacking direction and living only for today. Some appear disillusioned, others vague. Finding current societal conditions increasingly overwhelming, this stalwart in the community and school is contemplating joining her husband in the quasi-refuge of retirement. Those without Mrs. Ennis's strong sense of self barely subsist in a nonnurturing environment.

Erikson (1986) defines alienation in the context of one's connectedness to the external world—that is, having roots, a place to anchor and secure oneself. Problems wrought by massive economic and social inequities perpetuate a lack of integration among inner-city residents and the subsequent outcome of despair and desolation. Such conditions breed disconnectedness and disidentification, not only in relationships and interaction with others but in terms of self. Experiencing their own disconnectedness, poor inner-city parents must approach schools that unwittingly reinforce their hesitancy, fears, and self-defeating and self-defacing behaviors. They turn away, alienated in the rejection. A vicious cycle is perpetrated, invidious to all: parents, their children, and school personnel.

In a study of minority parents whose children are bused to a racially balanced, predominantly white upper-middle class elementary school in the Midwest, Calabrese (1990) comments that although parents in the study indicated a desire for meaningful interaction with school personnel, "they felt they lacked the personal knowledge or confidence to confront a large bureaucratic institution" (p. 151). Bounded by their uncertainties and insecurities, they avoided contact with the school and unwittingly reinforced the misguided assumptions of school personnel.

Only a small number of America's inner-city public schools are committed to developing processes to facilitate exchange and interaction between parents and schools. Mandates governing parent-school interaction, although meant to be enabling, can actually complicate the process. It is not the mandates per se but often the school's lack of knowledge and familiarity with the complexities of social interactions that becomes problematic. The social distance, sustained by the differences in race or ethnicity or class, is a major factor. For poor, ethnic, or minority parents whose children are more likely to experience dysfunction or failure in the educational process, the expectation that their presence is required takes on other dimensions affecting parents and school personnel alike. Trapped in the shackles of their own insecurities and fanned by the reality of negative feedback, these parents appear negatively disposed and disinterested. These negative attitudes are passed on to their children, affecting their sense of self, competence, and, ultimately, performance.

There are a number of principals and teachers whose responses run counter to the notion of alienating school personnel. Out of their own convictions, their day-to-day practices reflect how they value parents. Often without federal or state mandates and with minimal resources, they develop processes and activities and create an atmosphere that sends a positive though inconclusive message that parental input is important to the mission and goals of the school.

An individual can be an important catalyst in forging meaningful parent involvement. One of them is Judy Williams, appointed an elementary school principal in 1990 in Washington, D.C., following two decades that included work as a leader and proponent of parent involvement and a pioneer in Head Start programs. She held a variety of positions at the local level that put her in a position to garner school support, at both the local and administrative levels, for parent participation programs. Her commitment extends beyond programmatic endeavors to encouraging and mentoring mothers to develop skills they never knew they had. She is no longer directly affiliated with the many programs she was instrumental in instituting, but the legacy of her commitment is carried on by the large number of mothers who continue to be involved in the district's schools.

A majority of schools located in inner-city communities may inadvertently include in their invitation to participate the message that they have hesitancies and misgivings as to the role of parents, particularly in the on-site educational process (Chavkin 1989; Heid and Harris 1989). For many parents in these communities, this veiled message reinforces their own reluctance, insecurity, avoidance, and confusion regarding the formalities of organized education and their expected role. Surrounded by the congestion common to the ghetto, these parents suffer the isolation and loneliness associated with alienation.

Making Sense of the World

Meaninglessness, as a dimension of alienation, taps a mother's evaluation of her perception of her capacity to understand what is unfolding in a complex world. Mothers are asked whether they agree or disagree with the statement, "Things have become so complicated in the world today, I really don't understand just what is going on" (Srole 1956). The concept of meaninglessness connotes an individual's failure or inability to process information that ultimately is related to some future behavior or action. In contrast, a state of meaning prevails when the input is received and transforms existing perceptions, bringing about change in the individual's emotional state and how the environment is envisioned. Goals and values take on new meanings. When input or information is received, it is in turn altered by the individual's own cognitive structure and is received with a sense of respect, of being acknowledged and validated. Individuals are not viewed as passive recipients but are affected by and are capable of affecting their environment.

When the initial study was undertaken in the mid-1970s, America's black citizens were still imbued with the hope inherent in opportunity and the meaning related to a seemingly changing social and political terrain accompanying the momentum of the civil rights movement. Increased empowerment was visible at the polls, with sixteen African Americans elected to Congress. Coupled with this was the election of a number of black mayors in large cities such as Atlanta, Los Angeles, and New Orleans. Increasing participation of African Americans in mainstream political, educational, and economic institutions conveyed a message that blacks have a role in societal and global affairs.

By 1987, the social climate was less encouraging; the increasing decline in economic indicators marked a recession, and a number of educational and social programs had been cut back or eliminated, seriously affecting poor urban populations.

Yet in spite of the circumscribed, marginal, and often isolated lives of the urban black mothers, in the studies, high-participant mothers in both studies tended to disagree with the idea that they lacked the capacity to appreciate and act in behalf of or response to more global societal issues. The 1975 study demonstrates that mothers who are active participants in their children's school significantly negate the implication that certain events fall beyond the realm of their understanding. (See table A.1.) In neither study did demographic variables—education, age, marital status, spouse's employment, number of children, years in the neighborhood—have a significant effect on a mother's response to the statement targeting meaninglessness. And although education had no effect in the 1975 study, it surfaced as a primary factor in the 1987 study.

Education: Staving off Meaninglessness

In the 1987 study, analysis revealed that educational achievement is the most significant factor in influencing a mother's response to meaninglessness and, thus, her perception of how she views herself in terms of a capacity to understand and to act. This is in keeping with the concept of "locus of control" in psychology, which maintains that the higher the education, the more internally oriented and self-directed the individual. As such, these people believe they are responsible for what transpires in their lives. A number of studies cited already associate educational attainment with a decrease in alienation.

Of the 114 mothers, 3 identified themselves as college graduates, and another 14 had engaged in some college-level course of study. Those with some college education were five times more likely to reject the notion of meaninglessness than mothers who were not high school graduates. The gap narrowed as educational level increased: mothers with exposure to college education were three times as likely as those who were high school graduates to disagree with the idea that they could not understand or act upon information about societal events. (See figure 3.1.)

It is anticipated that as an outcome of the educational process, individuals will be able to perform tasks and process information that previously baffled them. An increase in knowledge, cognitive abilities, and skills enhances an individual's sense of competence and willingness to participate. In the interaction that occurs as an outcome of socialization and the educational aspect of participation, values are identified and redefined, approximating more dominant societal values. The exchange is ongoing, occurring in both formal and alternative modes of education.

Lowanda Henderson, a single mother of two children, applied for and received the position of school clerk following two years of active work in the school and participation in training programs. "Never in her wildest dreams" had she envisioned herself as a school employee. As a high school graduate, Lowanda was among the minority in this cluster of inner-city African American mothers with depressed educational status.

In an analysis of powerlessness and normlessness as indicators of alienation, education surfaces in some instances as the sole predictor of resistance to alienation, outdistancing a parent's participatory status.

The meaninglessness statement suggests for these mothers a social field that extends beyond that ordinarily defining the realm of their day-to-day responsibility. In responding to the inquiry as to what the statement seems to indicate to her, one inner-city mother, whose participation predated Head Start, couched the statement in the context of her own inclination to act. After a moment of pondering, she suggested that if by actions "you save one child, you have done a lot." In her voice, it is the "little things" that an individual can do, that "make a difference." She went on to note that if a child's frustration and anger in the lunchroom gets expressed in throwing his own food and dumping other children's food trays, time spent with this child not only calms this situation but conveys the message that someone cares. Annabell Stokes feels that "we can do something small" that can result in a positive outcome. In this mother's voice, it is not macro societal events that define her realm of potential but the effort she makes to intercede on a one-to-one basis. She interprets the statement in the context of empowerment, of what she can do about issues that touch her daily existence. Her expressed beliefs resonate with her persona. Her observing stance conveys her sense of purpose as she goes about fielding questions, giving directions to a child, and answering the principal's telephone in her secretary's absence. Mrs. Stokes stands firm in the aura of personal power.

Even among mothers with minimal and diminishing social support, the capacity to comprehend and ponder events beyond their daily existence remains. Another mother, when asked what concerns the meaninglessness statement evoked, speaks of "the drug deals that go down in the hallways of her building or right on the street in broad daylight." She speaks of her determination to keep her two boys, ages nine and ten, safe. Yet the doubt in her voice and eyes does not go unnoticed. Melody Jones does not let the boys out of her sight. She walks them to school and is waiting when school is dismissed. The street gangs frighten her, and she wonders, in an environment immersed in violence and drugs, "What will happen as my boys get older? Even the police can't seem to do anything." These mothers question the aid given to foreign countries when so many people in "our country don't have no place to live or jobs." They puzzle and envy the success of more recently arrived immigrants. Mrs. Stokes feels that "African Americans can learn a lot from the Koreans . . . They come here . . . can hardly speak the language . . . They stick together . . . they share. Many people will live in one small apartment. They pool and save their money and soon buy the house next door." The range of these mothers' responses suggests that their world is not defined solely in terms of the confines and demands of their daily lives.

Yet some mothers remain hampered by the hopelessness of years of welfare dependency and their being left alone to confront the daily responsibilities of living. Their frustrations and state of being overwhelmed can be observed in their interaction with school personnel and their children. In their impatience, they treat children more harshly than they would if circumstances were otherwise. Too many single, disadvantaged African American mothers appear to have resigned themselves to a stagnated existence. The essence of their being is intimately entwined with the desperation of their lives. Their children are viewed as an added burden, which they must endure. Their perceived world is defined by the reality of their persistent pain. Some succumb to the bitter comfort of defeatism, which subsumes initiative. Their sense of abandonment is pervasive. The behavior of some African American welfare mothers reflects such views. But a significant number refuse to fall victim to the demoralizing social forces and remain determined in their struggle to have a more gratifying life. Even some mothers who are identified as low-frequency participants are firm in their values and neither confused nor limited in what they understand about and seek in life.

Included in the concept of meaninglessness is the assessment of an individual's capacity to engage in planning activities and, in the process, to weigh and anticipate outcomes. Properties that can be cited as a mark of self-motivation or of a self-starter—one able to sustain individual effort toward goal attainment—are pivotal to this formulation. Through interaction with school personnel in planning and decision making, parents can gain skills associated with self-direction, such as negotiating and setting priorities and postponing gratification. Mothers who serve as classroom assistants or sit on executive planning committees or advisory boards, for example, share with principals and other school personnel the challenges of planning and accountability and the gratification that accompanies positive outcomes. Activities that engage and enhance performance and successful task completion give meaning to one's sense of self.

Doing What's Right . . .

Inner cities are becoming the breeding grounds of normlessness, the state in which any behavior is considered acceptable if it meets needs and fulfills goals. The urge for possessions is fanned by local role models and the electronic media. Unwittingly, members of the more privileged classes who have adopted the credo of acquisition serve as role representatives. This is not to suggest that the professional or middle class should temper the desire for achieving the "American dream." Rather, there is the responsibility for professional and national leaders to convey and develop the societal-sanctioned values that lead to acquisition. For many urban dwellers, the message that has been conveyed is, "possession by any means necessary." Illegal, marginal, or questionable behavior becomes acceptable, so long as the goal is obtained and needs are gratified. In the wake of urban violence and easy money, parents fear for their children's safety not only on the streets, in their travel to and from school, but for their safety when in school buildings. No longer are schools an undisputed place of refuge. Too often inner-city schools have become the battleground for brutally settled disputes. The drug trade is not limited to drug dealers or users. Young children are paid as runners or lookouts.

The question as posed, "In order to get ahead in the world today, you are almost forced to do some things which are not right" (Srole 1956), targets the basic issue of right and wrong.

One participant mother, an AFDC (Aid to Families with Dependent

Children) recipient who assists the kindergarten teacher almost daily, speaks of the normlessness concept in the context of demonstrations that occurred in a shopping center near her home. She was surprised by the number of her neighbors who joined in the melee and looting. Foodstuff, clothing, and electronic equipment were there for the taking. While some people tend to justify their behavior by pointing to the wrongdoings of the merchants, the police, the politicians, or an unfair system, her response is that "two wrongs don't make a right." Nodding in agreement, her participant counterpart agrees "I ain't got nothing, but I'm honest." Even with their marginal living conditions these mothers, including a sizable number of low-frequency participants, do not endorse illegitimate action or behavior to advance their lot in life. This is an important finding given the escalation of normless behavior in urban areas. The positive spirit and strength in these women with minimal comforts and pleasures in their lives remains intact. Yet, in our complex society with its mixed messages, the distinction between the acceptable and unacceptable is not always clear. Psychological strain results as individuals struggle in choosing between behaviors approved by the wider society and those that will fulfill a need.

Sociodemographic Factors and Adherence to Norms

Education

Educational level is a powerful determinant in predicting a mother's response to the alienation measures. A high educational level strongly influences a mother's inclination to follow and adhere to societal norms (figure 6.1). In some instances education is the major factor influencing differences in the response to normlessness, displacing participation. In an examination of the relationship to normlessness, education outweighs sociodemographic factors such as church affiliation, marital status, employment, and extended family configurations. Through the acquisition of knowledge and skills and competency development, educational experience generates a sense of autonomy and accomplishment. Individuals are able to exercise more independence in determining how they will behave or act, even when confronted with peer pressure. Task completion, a component of the educational process, gives a sense of accomplishment that serves to reinforce an individual's sense of competence. Educational experiences that are basic to the participatory process reinforce individualism, perseverance, and values that contribute to the good of the community. Mothers who are surrounded by the spoils of the drug trade retain their resolve to avoid the temptation, even when there is barely enough money for the necessities.

Figure 6.1. Education and Rejecting Normlessness

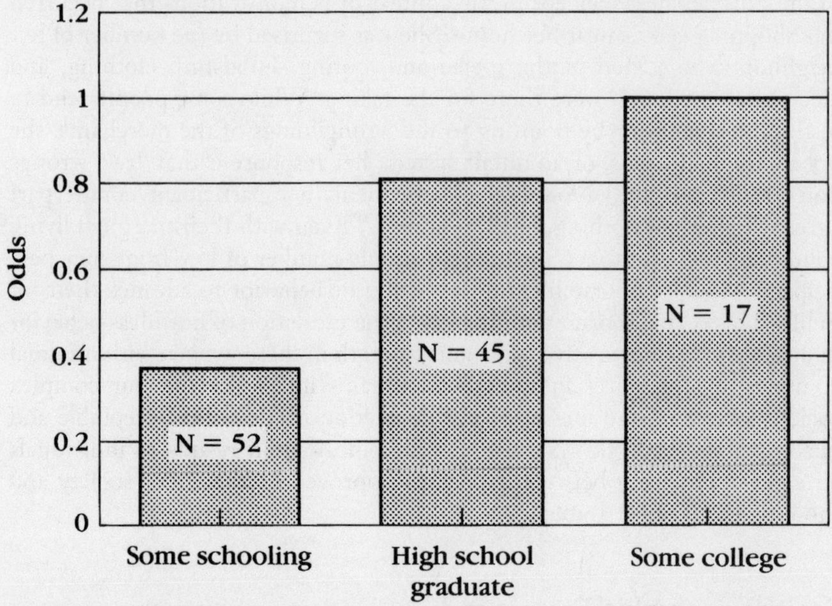

Note: Odds is the log of the ratio of the likelihood that an event will occur to the likelihood that an event will not occur.
Source: Table B.4.

Marital Status

Marital status surfaces as a critical factor in a mother's projected choices about what she would do in terms of acceptable and nonacceptable behavior. Nearly 50 percent of mothers in the 1987 study, have never married. Although the number of mothers who report being married is small, representing one-fifth of the total sample, analysis of their responses to the normlessness statement highlights the interaction of a mother's participant and marital status. The combination of these two factors is a powerful determinant in a mother's certainty that she would not resort to unacceptable means in order to make progress in her life. In focusing solely on the group of high-frequency-participant mothers, those who are married are seven times more likely to disagree with the idea that it is all right to do anything to achieve a goal than their high-frequency counterpart who is single (figure 6.2).

Normlessness suggests a social condition characterized by a paucity or lack of values. Societal-sanctioned norms have no relevance. Although this finding does not speak to the quality of the marital union, it does suggest that a living situation shared with a marital partner is related to a mother's rejecting the notion that any behavior is acceptable.

A number of the women in the study who had never married expressed

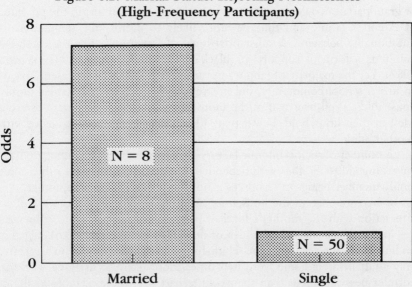

Figure 6.2. Marital Status: Rejecting Normlessness
(High-Frequency Participants)

Note: Odds is the log of the ratio of the likelihood that an event will occur to the likelihood that an event will not occur.
Source: Table B.5.

the desire for a mate—not only someone to share the responsibility of a child or children but someone who would stay around and be concerned about and care for them. These women were referring not only to care in the sense of meeting their daily needs but someone who would care what happened to them and would have their best interests at heart. Often these young women seemed to envision a prince charging in to rescue them from their dreary existence. Others recognized the reality of relationships but still thought it would "be nice to have someone who cared about me and the kids." Current social indicators do not hold out much hope for these young women; they forecast a bleak future in terms of marriage potential for more than a quarter of the black women between the ages of eighteen and thirty-four. A number of socioeconomic factors account for the demise of African American men as potential marital partners: low wages, unemployment, incarceration, and early and violent death. We hear the resentment and frustration of these women left sole responsibility for raising children. Throughout the nation, this number continues to rise; well over half of all African American children are being raised in homes by single women. The number of teenage mothers in America is reaching catastrophic proportions. Numerous accounts attest to the hardships that characterize these mothers' lives. Their families lack adequate housing, food, and medical care. They express resentment in having "to go it alone."

Given the anticipated benefit of shared responsibility, it was thought that mothers who had an additional adult in the home, such as an aunt, brother, or grandparent, would experience some support and comfort in the presence of extended family and thus be more likely to dismiss the temptation of questionable behavior. A substantial body of literature extols the extended family as a form of support for black family life (McAdoo 1981; Wilson 1987). Yet the majority of families in the study population, representative of an urban school community, did not reflect the pattern of extended family households. Well over half of the mothers reported that they were the sole adult in their household. Fewer than 30 percent shared their residence with another adult.

A number of socioeconomic factors are pertinent here, including policies governing aid to families with dependent children. Whether the other adult family member brings in resources is not the primary issue here; rather, it is his or her presence in the household. Another adult living in the home, in interaction with the mother's level of participation, significantly influences her inclination to decline the idea of normlessness (see table B.6). Yet this finding takes interesting form. High-frequency participants who were the only adult in their home were two times more likely to disagree with the normlessness statement than their counterpart with three or more adults in the home. Similarly, when high-frequency-participant status is held constant, mothers in households with two adults were eight times more likely to reject the idea of marginal behavior for personal gains than mothers in households with three or more adults. The data do suggest that the presence of the third adult does not appear to be a stabilizing factor in the context of mediating alienating responses. Only eight of the fifty-eight high-frequency participants were married, which would tend to minimize in-law conflict as a primary factor. Whether the adage "two's company, three's a crowd" is applicable, the finding does raise question about interactions in extended families.

Church Affiliation

When the initial study was undertaken in 1975, we wondered, after the fact, whether church affiliation would have effected any differences in the mothers' responses to the alienation statements. Of particular concern was the variant normlessness, which taps values, distinguishing behavior one deems as right and wrong. Given the strength and viability of the black church in black communities, we regretted not having obtained information regarding church affiliation.

In the 1987 study, church affiliation was defined in terms of the frequency of attendance at worship services or other church-sponsored events. Only 41 percent of both populations—twenty-four high- and twenty-three low-frequency participants—indicated church affiliation and attendance at least every other week. Slightly more than half (55 percent) of the low-frequency-participant group and slightly less than half (47 percent) of the high-frequency-participant group indicated no church affiliation. There was no significant difference in church affiliation between the two groups. Neither did regular association with a church have an effect on a mother's response to the alienation measures.

Employment

Given the demands and responsibilities of the workplace and home, one would anticipate that employment would tend to affect a mothers' accessibility for participation in school activities. What we did not foresee was the positive interaction between the status of a mother's employment and her participant status. A small portion, of this population (twenty women) were employed. Twenty percent of the low-frequency participants were employed compared to 14 percent of the high-frequency participants. About half of the mothers in both groups—seven in the low-frequency and four in the high-frequency-participant group—worked full time. Employed mothers whose participation in their children's school was characterized as high involved themselves in activities that exceeded the contact that is often limited to attendance at parent-teacher conferences or school meetings. In examining the effect of a mother's employment status in relation to how she viewed questionable behavior, employed high-frequency-participant mothers were twice as likely to disagree with the normlessness statement than their high-frequency counterparts who were unemployed (see table B.3).

The spontaneity of the conversation of these employed women was refreshing and hopeful, in contrast to the reluctant conversation of young mothers who were reticent and appeared to have relinquished any hope for the future. To say these mothers were satisfied with their wages and content with all aspects of their work would be an exaggeration, however. They decried low wages, complained about employee interaction, and wanted advancement. They spoke of inadequate transportation, the lack of adequate child care, and the tremendous burden for those who are trying to go it alone. The unreliability of child care especially influenced the quality of their lives. Yet in spite of their complaints and the tenuous quality of their lives, they nevertheless evinced a sense of relative well-being and the satisfaction of being self-sufficient. Employed in such work as a dietary aide in a public hospital, clerk-typist, or fast food restaurant worker, these mothers were committed to involvement in their children's school—"the only education my child will get," said one. These mothers appeared ready and determined to do their part to make it happen.

When first approached to volunteer, Fostina Walker did not see how she could juggle a job and help in school. Besides, what they were asking her to do—tutor or assist a teacher or contact parents whose children are absent— "that's what school people are being paid for." She discarded the notice that her son brought home requesting volunteers. Later, when attending an open school night, her curiosity was heightened as she heard parents report on some of the work they were doing in the school. She did not volunteer right away, but a few weeks later, after receiving several notices urging her to participate, she decided "to give it a try."

Fostina arrives at school about 3:45 P.M., after putting in a full day's work as a dietary aide. Her four-year-old son, whom she picks up from the sitter, is with her. Sometimes she assists in the after-school program her older son attends or volunteers on the telephone crew. As a member of the telephone crew, Fostina does not wait for children or families to call. The crew takes the initiative in contacting children to encourage and offer assistance with homework. Parents receive friendly reminders to see to it that their children complete their homework. Sometimes the telephone crew verifies attendance, reminds a parent of a scheduled appointment with the teacher or principal, urges parents to attend school programs, and asks them to consider volunteering themselves.

Since joining in these activities, Fostina Walker has been elected a member of the school's advisory committee that meets monthly to plan school activities and consider school issues. She never thought that she would be doing this and that her suggestions would be valued, as they are on the committee. Mutual benefits accrue from her interaction with school personnel. She brings a perspective and ideas that, when merged with those of professional and other lay members, strengthens school programming. A sense of well-being is fostered when she experiences her contribution as being sanctioned by others, especially those in authority. She admits that the responsibilities of work, raising her two sons, and volunteering are demanding, but she faces these challenges with increasing confidence.

Number of Elementary School-Age Children

Some interesting trends emerge concerning differences in the mothers' responses to normlessness when the number of children attending the schools in this study is taken into account. For mothers overall, as the number of children in the school increases, the more inclination to hedge in delineating right and wrong increases. Yet when the number of children a mother has attending the schools in this study is taken into account with her participatory status, those who are high-frequency participants are thirteen times more likely to hold to a determination to do what is right than low-frequency-participant mothers (see table B.7).

Mothers who had only one child in the study school were nine times more likely to disagree with the idea that it is all right to do anything in order to get ahead than mothers with three children. The ratio between those who agreed and disagreed decreased as the number of children attending the study schools increased. Mothers with two children were seven times more likely to disagree. Participation in school activities appears to be a potent force in mediating alienating features that may be related to family size.

As the number of elementary school-age children increases, so do the burdens and demands. A majority of these poor mothers struggle alone to provide food, shelter, and clothing for their children. When there are educational or social adjustment issues, the burden expands.

Aiesha Jones, the mother of three children, ages six, three, and thirteen months, described in chapter 3, speaks of the number of times she is summoned to the school because "some teacher doesn't like her child." She speaks of "being tired" of getting called in by different teachers. "I do the best I can ... I can't do no more." Her countenance and behavior are indicators of resigned indifference.

When there are educational or social adjustment issues demanding a parent's presence and cooperation, mothers such as Ms. Jones who are overwhelmed by the demands of their daily existence resist involvement. It is this kind of behavior that gives rise to the opinion held by a number of school personnel that disadvantaged parents are fundamentally uninterested in the education of their children. But for parents with minimal resources, the burdens increase as the number of children increase. When parents are destitute and lacking in competence, their children also manifest low self-esteem and an uncertainty that in turn negatively affects their educational performance.

In an ongoing program of parent involvement, we would anticipate that as the years of involvement increase, even with large numbers of children, the differences based on number of children would level off as mothers became more identified with the program and had favorable experiences that ultimately would have a positive effect on their resourcefulness.

Defying Powerlessness

In analyzing the 1987 data, both a mother's participant status and educational level significantly influenced how she responded to the notion of powerlessness. Education was the more significant factor. Mothers who had not completed high school were much less likely to disagree with the powerlessness statement than their more educated counterpart (figure 6.3).

A basic thesis of this book is that participation and its educational benefits contribute to personal development. When engaged in task-oriented activity with stipulated objectives and expected outcomes, the individual experiences his or her effort as being valued and accumulates strength that is generated by the realization that he or she is able to make things happen. In a society in which one is defined by what one does, a mother's identity and self-worth begins to be reaffirmed by virtue of her work in schools. We have

Figure 6.3. Education and Rejecting Powerlessness

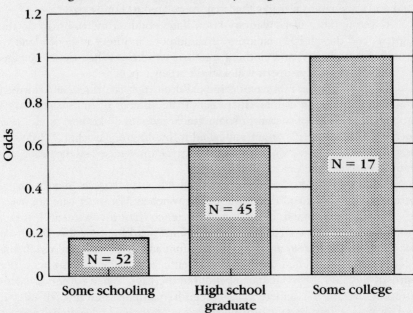

Note: Odds is the log of the ratio of the likelihood that an event will occur to the likelihood that an event will not occur.

Source: Table B.1.

observed the shift to more incisive behavior that occurs after a period of ongoing involvement in school-based activities. Mothers begin to recast and articulate goals related to their own development. This is a gradual process as skills are learned and confidence shaped. The measure of their commitment is found in the regularity and consistency of their attendance and their seeking out new assignments. The expressed interest in formalized study, either to qualify for the GED or for job training, comes later.

In the analysis of powerlessness, all interactions are eliminated. Although both a mother's participant status and education level make a significant contribution to understanding the variation of responses to the powerlessness statement, they do so independently of one another. Mothers identified as high-frequency participants were twice as likely to defy the implications of powerlessness as mothers whose participation was characterized as low (figure 6.3).

Participation: A Potent Force

Education in conjunction with a mother's level of participation plays a critical role in influencing responses to the powerlessness statement. Both formal education and the educational experiences related to the act of assisting in instructional or other school-related tasks serve important socialization functions, in addition to the acquisition of new knowledge and skills. Social skills are learned and developed that are transferable to other life situations. In the social system of the school, mothers learn to sort out and grasp the essence of social cues and behavior that will serve them well in other social situations. In interaction with school personnel and other mothers, they learn a range of coping behaviors. Educational experiences that are intrinsic to participation and involve investment of and proclaiming of self and the targeting of potential are compelling motivators. Through the education that occurs as a by-product of interaction in the participatory process, individuals are changed in critical ways.

Although a number of sociodemographic characteristics significantly affect a mother's ability to make sense of the world or influence whether she believes any behavior is fair game or alters her sense of powerlessness, participation looms large as both a primary and an intervening factor. When one takes part in an event or activity and assumes or shares responsibility for outcomes, accountability—the conviction that one is responsible for an outcome—becomes a critical dimension. There is personal investment in whether a project succeeds or fails. When accountability is extended, the message of anticipated competence is conveyed to those included. Assuming and carrying out new roles is a mark of a competent individual. A sense of competence is being nurtured as one satisfactorily performs in a status external to one's usual mode of operating. As a growth-producing experience, participation in schools can foster the development of or recapturing of strengths undiscovered or long dormant. Participatory experience emerges as a powerful force in redressing both personal and societal deficits.

Developing Responses to Educational Dilemmas

Involving parents is one response to the problems besetting urban schools. It is no panacea but a viable way to mitigate the distance between home and school prevalent in low-income areas. Amid the accumulating evidence regarding positive outcomes in student performance when parents participate in schools, there is still no national policy or implementation guidelines governing parent involvement in schools. This lack of leadership is grave.

America 2000 speaks to the primacy of the family in realizing the goal of educating the nation's children, but it does not address the needs of the poor or minorities and their children at risk. The directive fails to target explicitly those who are unable to negotiate the bureaucracy of the educational sector. The expectation that families defined by poverty, unemployment, incarceration, substandard housing, lead poisoning, substance abuse, and violence are capable of negotiating a complex educational bureaucracy to exercise their choice in school selection is unrealistic.

Public schools bear a great burden in responding to social problems besetting poor and minority families and children. One response to the educational inequities brought about by racially unbalanced neighborhoods and sustained by segregated housing is busing. Busing, however, increases the distance between school and home for poor and minority families. Some low-income parents accept busing, but others find the predominantly white middle- and upper-class suburbs foreboding and consider them foreign territory. These feelings persist in spite of suburban schools' special activities and programming for their nonresident populations. Perhaps unwittingly suburban residents claim the entitlement that accompanies ownership, sending this message to the visitors. The reality of bused children being relegated to less competitive educational tracks is a constant reminder of the intrusion.

Circumstances differ considerably in the Gautreaux program in Chicago, which moves low-income African American families to subsidized housing in the suburbs. As residents, these families and their children are part of and share ownership in the schools. The children's increased self-esteem and competence is evidenced by their academic performance, college admission, and high employment rate upon completion of high school (*Chicago Tribune* 1991).

Benefits for children, families, and schools can be realized by looking to models that have proved successful over time and modifying them to fit individual school needs. The educational sector is endowed with assets that can be utilized to create growth-producing environments for families and children. When parents and teachers work together, they create an atmosphere of mutual respect and empowerment and by so doing begin to interrupt the cycle of normlessness and alienation.

7
Participation: Searching for Self and Community

S earching for self and community identity are inextricably intertwined. Personhood flourishes on being anchored to the collectivity of the community. The development and fulfillment of the self becomes defined and realized in the context of relationships with others. For African Americans, community encompasses the mainstream society, as well as their own subculture. People take their soundings from their environment, seeking to establish an identity as a people. The devastating physical and social environment of the nation's urban areas inflicts psychological damage to individual self-esteem. Extending beyond the physical, this environment intrudes into the relationships and interactions that occur as individuals go about their daily business. A person's sense of worth, competence, and well-being can be strengthened or devastated in this interaction. Contaminated environments devoid of positive opportunities for involvement of self result in people's tendency to escape or isolate themselves. This can manifest itself in blatant disregard for societal imperatives, as is seen among those opting for the ill-gotten financial gains of the drug enterprise, which erodes their communities. Others who walk on the periphery of life barely manage to eke out an existence and remain only marginally involved. Still others turn to the seemingly protectiveness of isolation.

Social Isolation

Social isolation, another indicator of alienation, is manifested as a reaction of the self to escape a squalid environment by retreating within the perceived sanctity of the self. It refers not to the extremes of pathological withdrawal, as does self-estrangement, but rather to the limiting of connectedness. Interaction with wider society is minimized. For a large number of the mothers in this study, the fantasy of soap operas and the staged reality of television talk shows remain their primary connection with the wider society. There is little impetus for activity or involvement outside of confronting the demands of daily subsistence. Their own immediate community does not offer much solace or hope for establishing ties beyond the potential of the church. Many mothers overcome by the demands of caring for children alone on meager incomes have retreated to the solace of their own being. Their alienation borne of the social realities can be characterized as isolation of self as they adopt a social posture of inactivity.

The socioeconomic factors that account for much of the plight of urban communities continue to have a devastating toll on large numbers of poor and minority families. This is not to suggest, however, that individuals are entirely at the mercy of their environments. Some have the inner resources of discipline and determination required to battle encroaching societal forces, and increasingly they are taking up the gauntlet of change. Outcomes of their affirmation are seen in low-income housing ownership and management initiatives, neighborhood crime watch programs, and community-school partnerships that are having a positive effect on local communities.

Public schools remain a potential oasis of hope and refuge in the corroding inner cities. When parents are involved in on-site programs, schools have an opportunity to reaffirm wider societal goals by including parents. The lives of a number of African American mothers who participate in their children's school have been redirected and greatly enriched.

One Mother's Unfolding

In the 1970s Jackie Linnan struggled to care for her three elementary-school-age children. Mainly she kept to herself, a strategy that for years had offered some protection. Messages from the Balkin School urging her participation did not penetrate the protective barrier that she had created. She did not respond to specific invitations to join a group of parents in a meeting with the school social worker in the project community center. Upon learning that Mrs. Linnan walked her youngest to a point where she could keep an eye on her until she reached the school building, the school social worker planned to be in that location at the same time. As a result of their conversation, Mrs. Linnan indicated that she would attend a parent function scheduled the next day, but she did not.

It was another month before she attended a school workshop planned for parents. Two years after ongoing involvement in the school and regular interaction with the school social worker who coordinated the parent program, Mrs. Linnan revealed her initial uneasiness, remembering she did not know what to expect. She could not envision a role for herself; that thought made her uncomfortable and was disquieting, so she put it out of her mind. Jackie recalls that it was the school's steady stream of fliers, notices, and even notes pinned to her children's clothing that kept her in touch with up-and-coming events, although she still did not attend. After finally taking the plunge, Jackie remembers sitting apart from the other women, who all seemed to know one another. But before the workshop was over, another mother had asked her to work with her on a project that lasted for several weeks. Gradually, she began to feel more comfortable in the school. Other activities interested her, and by the following fall, she had made an ongoing commitment. Extremely gifted and hard working, Jackie assisted on the school newspaper and tutored individual children, although she had not been particularly understanding in assisting her own children with homework. Over the next year, her personal development progressed as her involvement increased. She took advantage of workshops and provided leadership for a major committee endeavor.

Motivated by the realization of her own competence, Jackie was intrigued by and subsequently put into motion the suggestion that she take courses at the community college. Three years later, she was awarded a scholarship in a baccalaureate degree–granting program. It took some negotiating by the school social worker to get the welfare department to include funds for child care in her monthly allowance. As she was nearing completion of her undergraduate degree, Jackie entertained thoughts of going on to graduate study. Her children were older and functioning better. She continued and received a professional degree in the early 1980s. Jackie revels in the joy of self-sufficiency. Today she is an empowered, dedicated professional, reaching out to children and families in the tradition of her experience. Her life is different, as have been the lives of her children.

Jackie's story is one of the many positive accounts that seem to pale in the wake of the human devastation wrought by today's inner-city environment. Through the exchange and interaction common to participation and ongoing socialization, she acquired knowledge, developed skills, and learned new attitudes. In the process, her ability and potential were reaffirmed. Education and participation interacted as significant determinants of Jackie's life chances.

Realizing Self-Sufficiency

Evidence suggests that self-sufficiency and initiative can develop from ongoing participation in on-site school activities in which there is the opportunity to interact with school personnel. Seeing the outcome of one's work, reflected in a child's glee in being able to master a computational problem or a task as simple as tying a shoelace, is gratifying. As an active participant and accountable, an individual is able to share in the joy of contributing to positive outcomes. In many ways, this fulfills the basic human need to be recognized and belong.

Ms. Malcolm experienced inner discord and physically withdrew when her insecurities were heightened and her inefficiencies exposed by her inability to handle the reading practice group. When she was assigned an activity in which she was competent and her skills utilized, her demeanor and relationship with the school were strengthened. The resulting positive outcomes benefited Ms. Malcolm personally, as they did the children. Self-realization and empowerment are by-products of successful task completion. One of the major ways a person is identified in American society is by what one does, one's work. For many of the mothers, the tasks undertaken in this model of participation are their work, albeit unpaid. In the process of assisting teachers as they carry out their responsibility, socialization is an essential product of the interaction with school personnel. Through working together, participants share the importance of fulfilling a duty. This outcome pertains for parents, school personnel, and children, whose increasing development and self-sufficiency further drive home the importance of the work. Each task successfully completed adds to an individual's self-confidence.

In a number of cases there are physical manifestations of change in self-perception. Ms. Malcolm's body language and gait changed from a hesitant, bedraggled stance to one representative of determination and purpose. In her step could be discerned her sense of direction. No longer did she hover at the edge of interaction. Instead, she sought out and suggested tasks that she might undertake.

Exposure and interaction with more self-directed peers effects changes in attitude and behavior in mothers. Particularly poignant and dramatic is the case of Angela Bryant, a homeless mother with two children who attend elementary school in a midatlantic city. Under the most adverse circumstances, Ms. Bryant persists in getting her children to school. School personnel marvel at the steps this homeless mother takes to avoid having her two children miss school. She is determined that they not be transferred from school to school as the family moves monthly from one shelter to another. From experience, she knows that their transfer papers will probably not catch up with them before they are required to change schools again. She achieves some stability by using a fictitious permanent address, but it means that she and the children must travel a complicated route involving a number of bus transfers so the children can attend the same school. She strives to bring some continuity to their lives. This mother's participation is different from that of many others. She teachers her children a valuable lesson of endurance and in the eyes of the adult world defies the stereotype of homeless persons. She touches bases and interacts with school personnel and other parents before making her rounds of the municipal agencies as she tries to bring some order into her chaotic life.

Accountability and Development of Self

An important aspect of taking part in on-site educational activities is that of accountability. When a mother becomes committed to an educational outcome, as she does when she assumes a task with a specified goal, she becomes accountable, accepting some responsibility for producing results. In the context of public education, that accountability is shared with school personnel as volunteers contribute to the educational process.

Accountability as a condition is not automatically evident. Outcomes are attributable to inputs. A sense of commitment is cultivated as the participating individual has a stake in the outcome. The task becomes merged with a person's very being, and the self becomes obligated to the sense of duty. Accountability comes about as a gradual process, reinforced by continued participation and other events in a person's life that call for or require commitment.

The intensity of obligation varies. Many of these parents' lives have been devoid of opportunities for the growth, development, and experiences that foster commitment. The first stages of implementing parent-school participation may belie any hope for the development of shared accountability. For example, when parents who volunteer repeatedly fail to appear during expected times and neglect to notify school personnel, discouraged, ambivalent, and perhaps even angry teachers and principals may understandably wish to pull back. When this occurs, volunteers can be reminded of their responsibilities in a manner that conveys the message that their contributions are missed and reinforcing the idea of shared accountability.

When Ms. Malcolm failed to keep her commitment to meet with the reading group, the classroom teacher persisted in attempts to contact her. Ultimately Ms. Malcolm responded to the repeated efforts to reestablish her connection with the school. This process can be burdensome, and classroom teachers, especially, need support and professional direction in handling parent volunteers who fail to follow through on a commitment and appear resistant. Often this emerges as the Waterloo in parent-school relations.

Accountability evolves as participation unfolds. Considered in terms of accountability to self, gratification comes of fulfilling a commitment. Realizing one's ability in the process of task completion, accountability includes willingness to extend oneself in a communal sense. The self-competent person can function fairly comfortably in a demanding community with the realization that the self can survive in interaction with other people, societal norms, and environmental forces. By virtue of sharing accountability with school personnel for educational outcomes and, by extension, with other parents and community members, an individual endorses the social value of commitment to others. The self becomes more stabilized in relation to others.

As an aspect of participation, shared accountability shifts the power and improves the basis for negotiation and understanding between those functioning within the social system of the school. This is particularly pertinent given the differences of educational achievement between school personnel and those who live in disadvantaged urban communities. Accountability serves a leveling function. Expectations on both sides are altered, changing the school's expectation and appreciation, as well as that of the parents. In the context of shared tasks and shared accountability, blame is reduced. As a valued stance, accountability is transferable to other experiences and interactions.

Joining together in common tasks and challenging experiences, parents, teachers, and other school personnel reap positive outcomes. Once parent-school interaction is stabilized, teachers, and principals treasure the experience, as evidenced in Comer's (1988) institutionalized School Development Program, the Central Park East Elementary School I in East Harlem (Schorr 1989), and the Schools Reaching Out program (Davies 1990). Moreover, the benefit extends beyond the school to the family and the wider community. This outcome is not immediate; rather, it comes of ongoing interaction with parents over an extended time, sharing in tasks together, learning from mistakes, and developing the trust that comes of working together toward shared goals. Both learn directly and indirectly from the other. The sense of responsibility that is cultivated carries over to these mothers' relationships with their own children. Shifts occur in how they perceive themselves in relation to involvement in their own child's overall functioning and school performance.

Values that derive from accountability, obligation, and satisfaction of task completion are potent allies in pursuing societal problems. Most pressing are the debilitating socioeconomic forces that are so destructive to the development of African American families and children. Although long-term national initiatives are required to undo the far-reaching damage to African American families, black men and women are obligated to join together to combat the myriad of social problems.

Regaining Community

The isolating effect of environments lacking in humane support and promise plays a primary role in the disintegration besetting the African American family, including the dissension occurring in black male-female relations. In nineteenth-century America, it was black males who were the spokesmen in the pursuit of legislation to protect black women in low-paying menial jobs who were the victims of physical and sexual abuse. Their voices were joined by black female activists who encouraged all black women to seek education and exploit political opportunities and other careers that would advance their lot in life (Terborg-Penn 1978). Historically, African American men and women labored together to right societal wrongs; they were united in their quest.

In the past twenty to twenty-five years, a weakening of the communal and political bonds between African American men and women has been sadly evident. More recently, African American men charge that black women's advancement in education and the workplace is at their expense. The anger and charges that should be directed at altering devastating societal forces are being deflected to an easier target. This anger and despair must be recast in a way that will be neither self-defeating nor destructive but ameliorative. To restore black family life, neighborhoods must be reclaimed and revitalized so that members of the community can turn to their neighbors for support and emotional sustenance. A sense of connectedness must once again prevail in desolate communities.

Belah and associates (1985) posit that a person's connectedness to others—in work, love, or community— is essential to personal fulfillment and well-being. The recapturing of community for African Americans must be done collectively by men and women. African Americans must quell the "many storms raging and winds blowing in Black male and female relations" (hooks and West 1991). The proliferation of the separatist discourse between African American men and women must be interrupted.

In view of this discourse, one could question why only black mothers are the focus of this study. Surely some black men are and have been involved in schools. Indeed, they are, as I indicated in the Introduction, although to a far lesser degree than are mothers. In the 1975 study, one male was a faithful member of the research team. In the 1987 Milwaukee pilot program, a number of dedicated African American males consistently tutored children in the after-school program or as mentors engaged children in enrichment activities outside of school. But most of them were employed professionals; only a few had children enrolled in the schools. Nevertheless, their commitment and dedication and the positive force they brought to the school benefited the students and school.

It is the reality that not only are there fewer viable black men in lower-income inner-city communities but involvement with schools, particularly in on-site activities, remains as traditionally viewed: largely a role fulfilled by women. Even with over 50 percent of women in the work force, women remain the primary caretakers of children. Tending to the demands of formal education is an extension of the parenting role, and given the realities of the 1990s, with the increasing number of single female-headed families, this role will continue to be carried out primarily by women.

In the 1990s, the number of births among single teenagers continues to rise. Many are bearing a second and third child. A disproportionate number of these young women are African American. Dash (1989) chronicles the informed and deliberate choice to have babies by girls as young as twelve and the calculated intent of adolescent boys to impregnate. Explanations for the escalating number continue to elude behavioral and social scientists. It has been suggested that for a large number of African American teenagers, having a baby affirms their identity and symbolizes their womanhood. For the teenage boys, fathering a child is a rite of passage symbolizing manhood. The future for these adolescent parents and their offspring is grim, even in the light of the number of school districts that sponsor high school programs for teenage mothers, in which child care and counseling is provided, and in special programming for teenage fathers. A critical phase of the lives of these young people, when they move from the dependency of childhood to the demands and responsibilities of adulthood, has been obliterated. Social and behavioral scientists are questioning not only the circumstances in which a generation of African American children are being conceived and raised but ponder the implications for future black family life.

The African American community alone cannot solve the problems besetting their own and other disadvantaged communities. Macro societal problems require macro societal solutions. However, resolution at the macro societal level alone is not enough. A variety of solutions must be directed to a number of levels. Successful program planning and implementation can no longer bypass or fail to include the grass-roots citizenry. At the local or community level, black men and women collectively can focus on improving certain aspects of societal problems, including the educational sector. Education has long been considered the primary factor in black advancement, and therein is a treasure trove of available expertise. Joining their professional colleagues, African American principals, teachers, and professional staff (social workers, psychologists, guidance counselors) can provide leadership in seeking solutions that address the needs of the less favored, both African American and other minority school children. A collective effort is required that generates thoughtful program planning in which males and females can experience success. For over a decade, James Comer's School Development Program (1980, 1985), individualized for each school community, has witnessed significant success in academic performance among African American boys and girls. Certainly the public school is a place where African Americans can continue to achieve positive outcomes, changing the nature of interaction.

The viability of African American families rests on a comprehensive effort that engages both men and women in recapturing community, and thus reaffirming and reshaping their existence. Community should be a place where compassion abounds and where individuals are valued for their uniqueness. In an earlier time, neighborhoods and localities were communities. But changing socioeconomic conditions have altered communities, both environmentally and psychologically. Community as a concept is more nebulous, residing in a number of places where bonding exists among individuals. Communities are the repositories of commitment, loyalty, and obligation (Belah et al. 1985). It is within communities that values are shared and behavioral patterns and traditions adopted. Schools as communities offer a vista of possibilities for children and families. Education remains a prime factor in this quest.

Outcomes for African Americans can be enhanced by seizing the opportunity for participation, particularly that available in public schools. African American mothers have benefited by discovering and rediscovering skills and abilities. A number have emerged with a keener sense of responsibility, commitment, and a fierce determination to improve their lot in life. They elect to further their education or seek employment training. These mothers find competence and hope in undertaking and mastering new tasks (Gilligan 1982). Their newly found strength is reinforced as they extend themselves in helping others. Flourishing in the growth possibilities and comfort in locating a niche for themselves in a nonnurturing wider environment, these mothers are defining who they are, charting their course, and embracing many challenges. They amass the personal power that comes with accountability. As poor African Americans, they have a critical role in the ongoing battle for an educational system that will sustain their sense of culture and community and teach the skills and competencies necessary for economic and political survival in mainstream America, which in turn is redefined by their participation. As contributing participants, these mothers have developed competencies and capabilities that can strengthen the educational process. School personnel can join with parents in creating a community of learning that enables the growth of children, parents, and teachers. The participation of parents leaves a positive imprint, an indelible image of empowerment upon the children's impressionable minds, the school, and all of society.

Appendix A
Alienation Item Responses, 1975

The following data are part of the parent evaluation of the Baldwin-King School Program in which 80 mothers were interviewed. Eighty mothers from an inner-city school of the same size, with comparable sociodemographic characteristics, served as the control. As part of the 55 item questionnaire, mothers were asked whether they agreed or disagreed with the three statements reflecting alienation (Winters 1975).

Table A–1
Distribution of Alienation Item Responses 1975

	Jones Street School Mothers			Baldwin-King School Program Mothers		
	Do not Agree	Agree	Total	Do Not Agree	Agree	Total
Powerlessness[a]						
Number of cases	36	44	80	36	44	80
Percentage	45.0	55.0	100	45.0	55.0	100
Normlessness[b]						
Number of cases	29	51	80	57	23	80
Percentage	36.2	63.8	100	71.3	28.7	100
Meaninglessness[c]						
Number of cases	21	59	80	31	49	80
Percentage	26.2	73.8	100	38.7	61.3	100

[a.] t value = 0.00.
[b.] t value = -4.71; df = 158; $p < .001$.
[c.] t value = -1.69; df = 158; $p < .05$.

113

Appendix B
Statistical Methodology and Tables 1987 Study

Teresa Williams, Ph.D.
Howard University

T he logistic regression model used in this study estimates the linear relationship between a dichotomous dependent variable and selected qualitative/categorical independent variables. The logistic model is expressed in log odds or odds. Log odds or logit is conceptualized as the log of the ratio of the probability that an event will occur to the probability that an event will not occur.

In the 1987 study, the question was whether the predictor model successfully distinguished between mothers who agreed or disagreed with the dichotomous dependent variables representing alienation.

The model chi-square is the difference between the −2 log likelihood chi-square with only a constant and the −2 log likelihood chi-square with the relevant variables and the constant in the equation. The degrees of freedom is also the difference between those obtained in the former analysis and those obtained from the full model. At successive steps, the model chi-square is determined by comparing the likelihood ratio chi-square of the previous step with that of the present step. This test is similar to the F test for the regression sums of squares.

The two predictor logistic models with meaninglessness, powerlessness, or normlessness as dependent variables are evaluated for significant model likelihood ratio chi-square, as in the following example.

Meaninglessness as Dependent Variable

The two predictor equations will always include participant status and one other classificatory variable. Participant status is coded 1 for high-frequency participant and 2 for low-frequency participant. Both main effects and interaction effects are included in the full model.

The predictor "highest grade obtained" is coded 1 for "some schooling,"

2 for "high school graduate," and 3 for "some college." The correlation matrix for participant status and highest grade obtained with the dependent variable Meaninglessness indicates correlations above .69 and as high as .72 between levels of the two independent variables. This suggests that the inclusion of both variables in the equation will result in significant multicollinearity. The backward regression selection results in a final model containing one term, highest educational level obtained, with a −2 log likelihood ratio of 8.430 with 2 degrees of freedom and a significance level of .0148. Since the observed significance levels are less than the cutoff value (alpha = .1) for removal, this term is retained. Thus, educational level accounts for a significant amount of the variation in the dependent variable Meaninglessness.

The model that follows provides some explanation of the relationship between educational level and the dependent variable Meaninglessness:

Variables in the Equation

Variable	B	S.E.
EXP(B)		
Educational level		
Some schooling	−1.6864	0.6112
0.1852		
High school graduate	−1.1891	0.6119
0.3045		
Constant	0.8755	0.5323

The coefficients for "some schooling" and "high school graduate" represent the change in log odds when each is compared to the high level, "some college." The negative values are associated with decreased log odds of the better outcome "disagreeing" with the statement about meaninglessness. The odds of changing from "agree" to "disagree" is less (.1852 to 1) for mothers with "some schooling" than for mothers who are "high school graduates" (.3045 to 1) in comparison to mothers who have some college education.

A classification table determines the fit of observed and predicted values. For example, a correct classification results if those predicted to agree with the statement on the basis of the model fall into the same cell as the observed cases who agree with the statement about alienation. The same is true for observed and predicted disagreement. The probability of falling into either group should equal .5. The extent of correct classifications is reported as a percentage.

The following classification table, on the basis of the model, helps assess how well the model predicts the actually observed values. The table is based on the probability that a mother has an equal chance of falling into either the "agree" or "disagree" category.

Predicted

	Agree	Disagree	Percentage
Observed			
Agree	62	5	92.54
Disagree	35	12	25.53
Overall			64.91

Sixty-two mothers are correctly predicted to agree with the "meaninglessness" statement, and five are incorrectly classified. On the other hand, twelve mothers are correctly predicted to disagree with the statement, and thirty-five are incorrectly classified. Overall, 64.91 percent are correctly classified. The table also indicates that mothers disagree with the statement at a greater rate than the model predicts.

Table B–1
Powerlessness, Education, and Participatory Status of Low- and High-Frequency Participants (LFP, HFP)

Term	Variables Remaining in the Equation			
	Log Likelihood	−2 Log LR	df	Significance of Log LR
Participant status	−71.233	3.468	1	.0626
Educational level	−75.520	12.043	2	.0024

Factor [Exp(B)] by Which Odds Change with a Unit Increase in Value of the Independent Variable			
Variable	B	S.E.	Exp(B)
Participant status (HFP compared to LFP)	0.7609	0.4103	2.1401
Educational level			
Some schooling compared to some college	−1.7466	0.6215	0.1744
High school graduate compared to some college	−0.5253	0.6215	0.5914
Constant	−0.4092	0.5903	

	Accuracy of Predicting Response Predicted		
	Agree	Disagree	Percentage Correctly Predicted
Observed			
Agree	48	14	77.42
Disagree	23	29	55.77
Overall			67.54[a]

[a.] An overall classification rate greater than 50 percent implies that the model is performing better than chance.

Table B–2
Meaninglessness, Education, and Participatory Status, Low- and High-Frequency Participants (LFP, HFP)

	Variables Remaining in the Equation			
Term	Log Likelihood	−2 Log LR	df	Significance of Log LR*
Educational level[a]	−77.255	8.430	2	.0148

	Factor [Exp(B)] by Which Odds Change with a Unit Increase in Value of the Independent Variable		
Variable	B	S.E.	Exp(B)
Educational level			
Some schooling compared to some college	−1.6864	0.6112	0.1852
High school graduate compared to some college	−1.1891	0.6119	0.3045
Constant	0.8755	0.5323	

	Accuracy of Predicting Response Predicted		
	Agree	Disagree	Percentage Correctly Predicted
Observed			
Agree	62	5	92.54
Disagree	35	12	23.53
Overall			67.54

[a.] The log likelihood (LR) ratio for the variable remaining in the equation is equal to the model chi-square.

Table B–3
Normlessness, Employment, and Participatory Status of Low- and High-Frequency Participants (LFP, HFP)

	Variables Remaining in the Equation			
Term	Log Likelihood	−2 LogLR	df	Significance of Log LR
Participant status	−70.336	1.216	1	.2701
Employment of respondent	−70.328	1.200	1	.2733
Participant status by employment	−71.779	4.103	1	.0428

	Factor [Exp(B)] by Which Odds Change with a Unit Increase in Value of the Independent Variable		
Variable	B	Sig	Exp(B)
HFP compared to LFP	0.4690	0.4270	1.5985
Employed compared to unemployed	0.7221	0.6646	2.0588
HFP by employed to HFP by unemployed	7.3969	21.3676	1630.9940
Constant	−0.3857	0.3144	

(cont.)

	Accuracy of Predicting Response		Percentage Correctly Predicted
	Predicted		
	Agree	Disagree	
Observed			
Agree	25	28	47.11
Disagree	17	40	70.18
Overall			59.09

Note: Model chi-square = 12.892; *df* = 3; significance = .0049.

Table B–4
Normlessness, Education, and Participatory Status, Low- and High-Frequency Participants (LFP, HFP)

	Variables Remaining in the Equation			
Term	Log Likelihood	−2 Log LR	df	Significance of Log LR
Educational level[a]	−78.949	5.099	2	.0781

	Factor [Exp(B)] by Which Odds Change with a Unit Increase in Value of the Independent Variable		
Variable	B	S.E.	Exp(B)
Educational level			
Some schooling compared to some college	−0.9956	0.5809	0.3695
High school graduate compared to some college	−0.2006	0.5917	0.8182
Constant	0.6061	0.5075	

	Accuracy of Predicting Response		Percentage Correctly Predicted
	Predicted		
	Agree	Disagree	
Observed			
Agree	31	24	56.36
Disagree	21	38	64.41
Overall			60.53

[a] The log likelihood (LR) ratio for the variable remaining in the equation is equal to the model chi-square.

Table B–5
Normlessness, Marital Status, and Participatory Status, Low- and High-Frequency Participants (LFP, HFP)

	Variables Remaining in the Equation			
Term	Log Likelihood	−2 Log LR	df	Significance of Log LR
Marital Status by participant status[a]	−78.949	4.959	1	.0259

	Factor [Exp(B)] by Which Odds Change with a Unit Increase in Value of the Independent Variable		
Variable	B	S.E.	Exp(B)
HFP by married compared to HFP by single	1.9823	1.0860	7.2594
Constant	−0.0377	0.1943	

	Accuracy of Predicting Response Predicted		
	Agree	Disagree	Percentage Correctly Predicted
Observed			
Agree	54	1	98.18
Disagree	52	7	11.86
Overall			53.51

[a] The log likelihood (LR) ratio for the variable remaining in the equation is equal to the model chi-square.

Table B–6
Normlessness, Number of Adults in the Home, and Participatory Status, Low- and High-Frequency Participants (LFP, HFP)

	Variables Remaining in the Equation			
Term	Log Likelihood	−2 Log LR	df	Significance of Log LR
Participant status by number of adults in the home[a]	−71.350	9.128	2	.0104

	Factor [Exp(B)] by Which Odds Change with a Unit Increase in Value of the Independent Variable		
Variable	B	S.E.	Exp(B)
HFP by one adult compared to HFP by three or more adults	0.6008	0.4316	1.8235
HFP by two adults compared to HFP by three or more adults	2.0939	0.8189	8.1165
Constant	−0.3895	0.2826	

| | Accuracy of Predicting Response Predicted | | |
	Agree	Disagree	Percentage Correctly Predicted
Observed			
Agree	31	19	62.00
Disagree	21	32	60.38
Overall			61.17

[a] The log likelihood (LR) ratio for the variable remaining in the equation is equal to the model chi-square.

Table B–7
Normlessness, Number of Children in Study School, and Participatory Status, Low- and High-Frequency Participants (LFP, HFP)

| | Variables Remaining in the Equation | | | |
Term	Log Likelihood	−2 Log LR	df	Significance of Log LR*
Participant status	−74.891	8.538	1	.0035
Number of children in the study school	−75.171	9.099	2	.0106
Participant by number of children in the study school	−74.084	6.923	2	.0314

| | Factor [Exp(B)] by Which Odds Change with a Unit Increase in Value of the Independent Variable | | |
Variable	B	S.E.	Exp(B)
HFP compared to LFP	2.5641	0.9755	12.9884
Number of children in study school			
One child compared to three or more	2.2074	0.8649	09.0919
Two children compared to three or more	1.9887	0.9015	07.3060
HFP by one child compared to HFP by three or more	−2.2074	1.1448	0.1100
HFP by two children compared to HFP by three or more	−2.8825	1.1788	0.0590
Constant	−1.8709	0.0137	

| | Accuracy of Predicting Response Predicted | | |
	Agree	Disagree	Percentage Correctly Predicted
Observed			
Agree	24	30	44.44
Disagree	11	47	81.03
Overall			63.39

Note: Model chi-square = 13.878; df = 5; significance = .0164.

References

Alden, John W. 1979. "Needed: A Broader Definition of Citizen Participation." In *Partners: Parents and Schools.* Edited by Ronald Brandt. Arlington, Virginia: Association for Supervision and Curriculum Development.

Babchuck, N., and Thompson, R. 1962. "Voluntary Association of Negroes." *American Sociological Review* 27:647–55.

Belah, Robert N.; Madsen, Richard; Sullivan, William M.; Swidler, Ann; and Tipton, Steven M. 1985. *Habits of the Heart: Individualism and Commitment in American Life.* New York: Harper & Row.

Bell, W., and Force, M. 1956. "Urban Neighborhood Types and Participation." *American Sociological Review* 21:25–34.

Bengtson, Vern; Grigsby, Eugene; Corry, Elaine; and Hruby, Mary. 1977. "Relating Academic Research to Community Concerns: A Case Study in Collaborative Effort." *Journal of Social Issues* 33:75–92.

Berger, Eugenia H. 1981. *Parents as Partners in Education: The School and Home Working Together.* St. Louis: C. V. Mosby Co.

Blackwell, James E. 1985. *The Black Community: Diversity and Unity.* 2d ed. New York: Harper & Row.

Blauner, R., and Wellman, D. 1973. "Toward the Decolonization of Social Research." In *The Death of White Sociology.* Edited by J. A. Ladner. New York: Vintage.

Bogart, Joanne, and Le Tendre, Mary Jean. 1991. "Keeping Homeless Children in School." *PTA Today* 16:23–24.

Braddock, Jomills H. II. 1985. "School Desegregation and Black Assimilation." *Journal of Social Issues* 41:9–22.

Braden, William 1991. "Children from Projects Thrive in Suburbs-Study." *Chicago Sun-Times*, October 9, pp. 1, 32.

Bradley, David. 1981. *The Chaneyville Incident.* New York: Harper & Row.

Brandt, Allan M. 1978. "Racism and Research: The Case of the Tuskegee Syphilis Study." *Hastings Center Report* 8:21–29.

Bredo, Anneke E., and Bredo, Eric R. 1975. "Effects of Environment and Structure on the Process of Innovation." In *Managing Change in Educational Organizations: Sociological Perspectives, Strategies and Case Studies.* Edited by J. Victor Baldridge and Terrence Deal. Berkeley, California: McCutchan Publishing Corporation.

Brim, Orville. 1965. *Education for Child Rearing*. New York: Free Press.

Bullough, B. 1967. "Alienation in the Ghetto." *American Sociological Review* 72:469–78.

Calabrese, Raymond L. 1990. "The Public School: A Source of Alienation for Minority Parents." *Journal of Negro Education* 59:148–54.

Carlson, Richard O. 1975. "Environmental Constraints and Organizational Consequences: The Public School and Its Clients." In *Managing Change in Educational Organizations: Sociological Perspectives, Strategies and Case Studies*. Edited by J. Victor Baldridge and Terrence Deal. Berkeley, California: McCutchan Publishers.

Chavkin, Nancy F. 1989. "Debunking the Myth About Minority Parents." *Educational Horizons* 67:119–23.

Chilman, C. *Growing Up Poor*. 1966. Washington, D.C.: U.S. Government Printing Office.

Clark, G. 1959. "Measuring Alienation Within a Social System." *American Sociological Review* 24:849–52.

Cloward, R., and Jones, J. 1963. "Social Class: Educational Attitudes and Participation." In *Education in Depressed Areas*. Edited by A. H. Passow. New York: Bureau of Publications, Teachers College, Columbia University.

Coleman, J.; Campbell, E. Q.; Hobson, C. J.; McPartland, J.; Mood, A. M.; Weinfeld, F. D.; and York, R. L. 1966. *Equality of Educational Opportunity*. Washington, D.C.: U.S. Government Printing Office.

Comer, James P. 1980. *School Power*. New York: Free Press.

———. 1985. "The Yale–New Haven Primary Prevention Project: A Follow-up Study." *Journal of the American Academy of Child Psychiatry*. 24:154–60.

———. 1986. "Parent Participation in the Schools." *Phi Delta Kappan* (February): 442–46.

———. 1988. "Is 'Parenting' Essential to Good Teaching." *NEA Today* 6:34–40.

———. 1989. "Poverty, Family and the Black Experience." In *Giving Children a Chance: The Case for More Effective National Policies*. Washington, D.C.: Center for National Policy Press.

Costello, Joan. 1973. "Research in a Black Community: Four Years in Review." *School Review* 81:487–500.

Dahl, Robert A. 1961. *Who Governs? Democracy and Power in an American City*. New Haven, Conn.: Yale University Press.

Dash, Leon. 1989. *When Children Want Children: The Urban Crises of Teenage Childbearing*. New York: William Morrow and Co.

Davies, Don. 1976. *Schools Where Parents Make a Difference*. Boston: Institute for Responsive Education.

———, with Clasby, Miriam; Zerchykov, Ross; and Powers, Brian. 1978. *Patterns of Citizen Participation in Educational Decision Making*. Vol. 1. Boston: Institute for Responsive Education.

———. 1990. "Shall We Wait for the Revolution? A Few Lessons from the Schools Reaching Out Project." *Equity and Choice* 6:68–73.

Dean, Dwight. 1961. "Alienation: Its Meaning and Measurement." *American Sociological Review* 26:753–58.

DeFrancis, Marc. 1991. "Growing Up with Less." *Focus* 19:7.

Dewey, John. 1927. *The Public and Its Problems*. New York: Holt.

Durkheim, Emile. 1951. *Suicide: A Study in Sociology*. Translated by J. A. Spaulding and G. Simpson. New York: Free Press.

Edelman, Marion W. 1988. "An Advocacy Agenda for Black Families and Children." In *Black Families*. Edited by H. P. McAdoo. Newbury Park, Calif.: Sage.

Elkins, Stanley, and McKitrick, Eric. 1954. "A Meaning for Turner's Frontier Part I: Democracy in the Old Northwest." *Political Science Quarterly* 69:321–53.

Epstein, Joyce. 1991. "Paths to Partnership: What We Can Learn from Federal, State, District, and School Initiatives." *Phi Delta Kappan* (January): 334–49.

Erikson, Eric. 1968. *Identity, Youth, and Crisis*. New York: W. W. Norton and Company.

Erikson, Kai. 1986. "On Work and Alienation." *American Sociological Review* 51:1–8.

Etzioni, Amitae. 1968. "Basic Human Needs: Alienation and Inauthenticity." *American Sociological Review* 33:870–75.

Fantini, Mario D. 1974. *What's Best for the Children: Resolving the Power Struggle Between Parents and Teachers*. Garden City, N.Y.: Anchor Press/Doubleday.

Fruchter, N. 1984. "The Role of Parent Participation." *Social Policy* 15:32–36.

Germain, Carel B. 1988. "School as a Living Environment Within the Community." *Social Work in Education* 10:260–76.

Germain, Carel B., and Gitterman, Alex. 1980. *The Life Model of Social Work Practice*. New York: Columbia University Press.

Geyer, R. Felix, 1980. *Alienation Theories: A General Systems Approach*. New York: Pergamon Press.

Gilligan, Carol. 1982. *In a Different Voice: Psychological Theory and Women's Development*. Cambridge, Massachusetts: Harvard University Press.

Gittel, Marilyn. 1978. "Participation or Co-optation: A Look at Mandated Participation." *Citizen Action in Education* 5:5–6.

Gladwin, Thomas. 1967. "Social Competence and Clinical Practice." *Psychiatry* 80:30–43.

Glasgow, Douglas G. 1980. *The Black Underclass*. New York: Vintage Books.

Glasgow-Winters, Wendy R. 1976. "Negotiated Research: Grassroot Alternative to Alienation." In *Contemporary Topics in Alienation*. Edited by R. Bryce Laporte and C. Thomas. New York: Praeger Press.

Glazer, Nathan. 1988. *The Limits of Social Policy*. Cambridge, Mass.: Harvard University Press.

Goldring, Ellen B. 1990. "Principals' Relationship with Parents: The Homogeneity Versus the Social Class of the Parent Clientele." *The Urban Review* 22:1–15.

Gordon, Ira. 1977. "Parent Education and Parent Involvement." *Childhood Education* 54:71–79.

Greenberg, Edward. 1975. "The Consequences of Worker Participation: A Clarification of the Theoretical Literature." *Social Science Quarterly* 56:191–209.

Hall Johnson Series of Negro Spirituals. 1946. New York: G. Schirmer.

Heid, Camilla, and Harris, J. John III. 1989. "Parent Involvement: A Link Between Schools and Minority Communities." *Community Education Journal* 16:26–28.

Henderson, A. 1987. *The Evidence Continues to Grow: Parent Involvement Improves Student Achievement*. Columbia, Md.: National Committee for Citizens in Education.

hooks, bell and West, Cornell. 1991. *Breaking Bread: Insurgent Black Intellectual Life*. Boston, Massachusetts: South End Press.

Horton, J. 1964. "Dehumanization of Anomie and Alienation: A Problem in the Ideology of Sociology." *British Journal of Sociology* 15:283–300.

Hougland, James. 1988. "Criteria for Client Evaluation of Public Programs: A Comparison of Objective and Perceptual Measures." *Social Science Quarterly* 68:386–94.

Hyman, Herbert. 1971. "Trends of Voluntary Association Memberships of American Adults: A Replication Based on Secondary Analysis of National Sample Surveys." *American Sociological Review* 36:191–206.

Inkeles, Alex. 1966. "Social Structure and the Socialization of Competence." *Harvard Educational Review* 36:265–83.

Jackson, James S.; Tucker, M. Belinda; and Bowman, Phillip J. 1982. "Conceptual and Methodological Problems in Survey Research on Black Americans." In *Methodological Problems in Minority Research*. Edited by W. T. Liu. Chicago: Pacific/Asia American Mental Health Research Center.

Janowitz, Morris, and Marvick, Dwaine. 1956. *Competitive Pressures and Democratic Consent*. Michigan Governmental Studies, no. 32. Ann Arbor: University of Michigan Press.

Jenkins, Percy W. 1981. "Building Parent Participation in Urban Schools." *Principal* 61:20–23.

Johnson, Vivian R. 1990. "Schools Reaching Out: Changing the Message to 'Good News.'" *Equity and Choice* 6:20–24.

Johnston, Marilyn, and Slotnik, Joanne. 1985. "Parent Participation in the Schools: Are the Benefits Worth the Burdens?" *Phi Delta Kappan* 66:430–33.

Josephson, Eric. 1970. "Resistance to Community Surveys." *Social Problems* 18:117–29.

Kamarovsky, M. 1946. "The Voluntary Associations of Urban Dwellers." *American Sociological Review* 11:686–98.

Keene, Karlyn, and Ladd, Everett. 1990. "Public Opinion Report." *American Enterprise* 1:103–12.

Keniston, Kenneth. 1965. *The Uncommitted: Alienated Youth in America*. New York: Harcourt, Brace and World.

Kosters, Marvin H. 1990. "Be Cool Stay in School." *American Enterprise* 1:60–61.

Kozol, Jonathan. 1991. *Savage Inequalities: Children in America's Schools*. New York: Crown Publishers.

Kreuziger, Robert. 1986. "Annual Summary of Activities in Parent/School Collaboration Project at Lee School in 1985–86." Mimeographed. Milwaukee Public Schools.

Lewin, Kurt; Lippett, Ronald; and White, Ralph. 1939. "Patterns of Aggressive Behavior in Experimentally Designed Social Climates." *Journal of Social Psychology* 10:271–99.

Lightfoot, Sara L. 1978. *Worlds Apart: Relations Between Families and Schools*. New York: Basic Books.

Litwak, Eugene, and Meyer, Henry J. 1974. *School, Family and Neighborhood: The Theory and Practice of School-Community Relations*. New York: Columbia University Press.

London, Bruce. 1975. "Racial Differences in Social and Political Participation: It's Not Simply a Matter of Black and White." *Social Science Quarterly* 56:274–86.

Lopate, C.; Flaxman, E.; Bynum, E.; and Gordon, E. 1970. "Decentralization and Community Participation in Public Education." *Review of Educational Research* 40:135–48.

Lucas, J. G. 1985. "The Social Participation of Blacks: A Proposed Synthesis of Two Competing Theories." *Sociological Inquiry* 55:97–108.

Lystad, M. 1972. "Social Alienation: A Review of Current Literature." *Sociological Quarterly* 13:90–113.

McAdoo, Harriette. 1981. *Black Families.* Beverly Hills: Sage.

Maluccio, Anthony N. 1981. *Promoting Competence in Clients: A New/Old Approach to Social Work Practice.* New York: Free Press.

Marcus, F. F. 1984. "A Blend of Parents and Teachers." *New York Times*, April 15, pp. 38–39.

Marin, Gerardo, and Marin, Barbara VanOss. 1991. *Research with Hispanic Populations.* Applied Social Research Series, vol. 23. Newbury Park, Calif.: Sage.

Marriott, Michel. 1990. "A New Road to Learning: Teaching the Whole Child." *New York Times*, June 13, pp. A1, B7.

Martineau, William H. 1976. "Social Participation and a Sense of Powerlessness Among Blacks: A Neighborhood Analysis." *Sociological Quarterly* 17:27–41.

Marx, Karl. 1964. [1844]. "Economic and Philosophical Manuscripts," in *Karl Marx Early Writings.* Edited and translated by Thomas B. Bottomore. New York: McGraw-Hill Company.

Mechanic, David. 1974. "Social Structure and Personal Adaptation: Some Neglected Dimensions." In *Coping and Adaptation.* Edited by George V. Coelho, David Hambury, and John E. Adams. New York: Basic Books.

Mennerick, Lewis A. and Najafizadeh, Mehrangiz. 1987. "Observations of the Missing Linkage Between Theories of Historical Expansion of Schooling and Planning for Future Educational Development." *International Education* 33.

Merton, Robert K. 1972. "Insiders and Outsiders: A Chapter in the Sociology of Knowledge." *American Journal of Sociology* 78:9–48.

———. 1968. *Social Theory and Social Structure.* 3d ed. New York: Free Press.

———. 1957. "Continuities in the Theory of Social Structure and Anomie." In *Social Theory and Social Structure.* Rev. ed. Glencoe, Illinois: Free Press.

Middleton, Robert. 1963. "Alienation, Race and Education." *American Sociological Review* 28:973–77.

Milwaukee Journal. 1986. September 14, p. 7A.

Mobley, Marilyn E. 1987. "Narrative, Dilemma: Jadine as Cultural Orphan in Toni Morrison's Tar Baby." *Southern Review* 23:761–70.

Mogulof, M. 1973. "Citizen Participation: Federal Policy." In *Perspectives in Urban America.* Edited by Melvin Urofsky. Garden City, N.Y.: Anchor Press/Doubleday.

Morrison, George S. 1978. *Parent Involvement in the Home, School and Community.* Columbus, Ohio: Charles E. Merrill Publishing Co. and Bell and Howell Co.

Moynihan, Daniel P. 1965. *The Negro Family: The Case for National Action.* Washington, D.C., Office of Policy and Planning and Research, U.S. Department of Labor.

Murphy, K. 1990. "The Education Gap Rap." *American Enterprise* 1:62–63.

Narvaez, Alfonso A. 1984. "Parents' Mops and Paints Save School." *New York Times*, April 15, p. 38.

National Center for Education Statistics. 1990. *Dropout Rates in the United States: 1989.* Washington, D.C.: U.S. Department of Education.

National Commission on Excellence in Education. 1983. *A Nation at Risk: The Im-*

perative for Educational Reform. Washington, D.C.: U.S. Department of Education.

New York Times. 1990. June 13, p. B7.

Ogbu, John. 1988. "Cultural Diversity and Human Development." In *Black Children and Poverty: A Developmental Perspective.* Edited by D. T. Slaughter. New Directions for Child Development Series, no. 42. San Francisco: Jossey-Bass.

———. 1978. *Minority Education and Caste: The American System in Cross-Cultural Perspective.* New York: Academic Press.

Olsen, Marvin. 1970. "Social and Political Participation of Blacks." *American Sociological Review* 35:682–97.

———. 1972. "Social Participation and Voting." *American Sociological Review* 37:317–33.

Orum, A. 1966. "A Reappraisal of the Social and Political Participation of Negroes." *American Journal of Sociology* 72:32–46.

Parker, F. L.; Piotrkowski, C.S.; and Peay, L. 1987. "Head Start as a Social Support for Mothers: The Psychological Benefits of Involvement." *American Journal of Orthopsychiatry* 57:220–33.

Pateman, Carole. 1970. *Participation and Democratic Theory.* New York: Cambridge University Press.

Pennekamp, Marianne, and Freeman, Edith M. 1988. "Toward a Partnership Perspective: Schools, Families, and School Social Workers." *Social Work in Education* 10:246–59.

Phi Delta Kappan. 1980. "Why Do Some Urban Schools Succeed?" Phi Delta Kappan Study of Exceptional Urban Elementary Schools, Indiana.

Philips, W. M., Jr. 1975. "Conflict, Adaptive Community Organization, and Educational Participation." Paper read at the Annual Meeting of the American Educational Research Association, Washington, D.C.

P.T.A. Today. 1991. vol. 16 (4).

Ravitch, Carol M. 1974. *The Great School Wars: New York City 1805–1973: A History of the Public Schools as a Battlefield of Social Change.* New York: Basic Books.

Rexroat, Cynthia. 1990. *The Declining Economic Status of Black Children.* Washington, D.C.: Joint Center for Political and Economic Studies.

Richardson, Lynda. 1991. "D.C.'s Principal Attribute." *Washington Post,* October 24, pp. D.C.1, D.C.8.

Rist, Ray C. 1970. "Student Social Class and Teacher Expectations: The Self-Fulfilling Prophecy in Ghetto Education." *Harvard Education Review* 40:411–51.

Rosenberg, G. 1984. "In the South Bronx: A Dramatic Rebirth." *New York Times,* April 15, pp. 44–66.

Sarason, Seymour. 1982. *The Culture of the Schools and the Problem of Change.* 2d edit. Boston: Allyn and Bacon.

Schaff, Adam. 1980. *Alienation as a Social Phenomenon.* New York: Pergamon Press.

Schacht, Richard. 1970. *Alienation.* Garden City, N.Y.: Doubleday.

Schorr, Lisbeth B., with Schorr, Daniel. 1988. *Within Our Reach.* Garden City, N.Y.: Anchor Press/Doubleday.

Schraft, Carol M. 1978. "Developing Parent Participation Programs in Schools." Paper read at the New York State Social Work Conference.

Seeman, Melvin. 1959. "On the Meaning of Alienation." *American Journal of Sociology* 24:783–91.

———. 1983. "Alienation Motifs in Contemporary Theorizing: The Hidden Continuity of the Classic Themes." *Social Psychology Quarterly* 46:171–84.

Silverman, Charles. 1970. *Crisis in the Classroom*. New York: Random House.

Slaughter, Diana T., ed. 1988. "Black Children, Schooling, and Educational Intervention." In *Black Children and Poverty: A Developmental Perspective*. New Directions for Child Development Series, no. 42. San Francisco: Jossey-Bass.

Smith, Brewster M. 1968. "Competence and Socialization." In *Socialization and Society*. Edited by John A. Clausen. Boston: Little, Brown.

Sommer, Robert. 1987. "An Experimental Investigation of the Action Research Approach." *Journal of Applied Behavioral Science* 23:185–99.

Srole, Leo. 1956. "Social Integration and Certain Corrolaries: An Exploratory Study." *American Sociological Review* 21:709–716.

Swap, Susan McAllister. 1990. "Comparing Three Philosophies of Home-School Collaboration." *Equity and Choice* 6:9–19.

Taviss, I. 1969. "Changes in the Form of Alienation: The 1960's vs. the 1950's." *American Sociological Review* 34:46–57.

Taylor, Paul. 1991. *Washington Post*, January 22, p. A3.

Terborg-Penn, Roslyn. 1978. "Discrimination Against Afro-American Women in the Women's Movement, 1830–1920." In *The Afro-American Woman: Struggles and Images*. Edited by S. Harley and R. Terborg-Penn. Port Washington, N.Y.: Kennikat Press Group.

Theodorson, George A., and Theodorson, Achilles G. 1969. *A Modern Dictionary of Sociology*. New York: Thomas Y. Crowell Co.

Thibault, André. 1981. "Studying Alienation Without Alienating People: A Challenge for Sociology." In *Alienation: Problems of Meaning, Theory and Method*. Edited by R. Felix Geter and David Schweitzer. Boston: Routledge and Kegan Paul.

Travis, Robert. 1986. "On Powerlessness and Meaninglessness." *British Journal of Sociology* 37:61–73.

U.S. Bureau of Labor Statistics. 1992. *Current Population Survey 1992 Annual Averages*. Washington, D.C.: U.S. Government Printing Office.

U.S. Bureau of the Census. 1990. "Educational Attainment in the U.S.: March 1989 and 1988." *Current Population Report*, Series P-20. Washington, D.C.: U.S. Government Printing Office.

U.S. Commission on Higher Education. 1974. *Higher Education for American Democracy*. Washington, D.C.: U.S. Government Printing Office.

U.S. Department of Education. 1991. *America 2000*. Washington, D.C.: U.S. Government Printing Office.

Urofsky, M. 1973. *Perspectives on Urban America*. Garden City, N.Y.: Anchor Press/Doubleday.

Wasserman, Sidney. 1979. "Ego Psychology." In *Social Work Treatment: Interlocking Therapeutic Approaches*. Edited by Francis Turner. New York: Free Press.

West, Earle H. 1972. *The Black American and Education*. Columbus, Ohio: Charles E. Merrill.

White, Robert. 1974. "Strategies of Adaptation: An Attempt at Systematic Description." In *Coping and Adaptation*. Edited by George V. Coelho, David A. Hamburg, and John E. Adams. New York: Basic Books.

———. 1963. *Ego and Reality in Psychoanalytic Theory*. New York: International Universities Press.

————. 1959. "Motivation Reconsidered: The Concept of Competence." *Psychological Review* 66:297–333.

Williams, J. A.; Babchuk, N.; and Johnson, D. R. 1973. "Voluntary Associations and Minority Status: A Comparative Analysis of Anglo, Black and Mexican Americans." *American Sociological Review* 58:637–46.

Willie, Charles. 1968. "Education, Deprivation and Alienation." *Journal of Negro Education* 34:209–19.

Wilson, William J. 1987. *The Truly Disadvantaged: The Inner City, the Underclass and Public Policy.* Chicago: University of Chicago Press.

Wiltz, Teresa. 1991. "In Seeking Better Life, Location Key, Study Says." *Chicago Tribune*, October 9, pp. 1, 10.

Winters, Wendy Glasgow. 1975. "Black Mothers in Urban Schools: A Study of Participation and Alienation." Ph.D. dissertation, Yale University.

Winters, Wendy, and Easton, Freda. 1983. *The Practice of Social Work in Schools: An Ecological Perspective.* New York: Free Press.

Winters, Wendy, and Maluccio, Anthony. 1988. "School, Family, and Community: Working Together to Promote Social Competence." *Social Work in Education* 10:207–17.

Zeldin, Shepherd. 1990. "The Implementation of Home-School-Community Partnerships: Policy from the Perspective of Principals and Teachers." *Equity and Choice* 6:56–63.

Zigler, Edward. 1985. "Assessing Head Start at 20: An Invited Commentary." *American Journal of Orthopsychiatry* 55:603–9.

Zigler, E., and Valentine, J., eds. 1979. *Project Head Start: A Legacy of the War on Poverty.* New York: Free Press.

Zinn, Maxine Baca. 1979. "Field Research in Minority Communities: Ethical Methodological and Political Observations by an Insider." *Social Problems* 27:209–19.

Index

131